FUNNY YOU SHOULD THINK ABOUT A RETURN TO JUDAISM

A Journey From Comedy Stages
to the Wisdom of Sages

FUNNY YOU SHOULD THINK ABOUT A RETURN TO JUDAISM

A Journey From Comedy Stages to the Wisdom of Sages

by Richard Morris

Forward Focus Publishing
New York

Funny You Should Think
About a Return to Judaism

A Journey From Comedy Stages to the Wisdom of Sages

copyright © 2013
by
Richard Morris
www.richardmorrisworks.com
info@richardmorrisworks.com

ISBN-13: 978-0-9889759-0-3

Special Thanks to:
Editor, Zhanna Vaynberg
Interior Designer, Barbara Hodge
Proofreader, Genevieve Salazar

Cataloging-in-Publication data for this book is available upon request.

Forward Focus Publishing
New York

Contents

Acknowledgments

There are not enough words to thank all the people who were instrumental in my return to my Judaism, many of whom are mentioned in this book. I'd like to especially thank Rabbis Ephraim Buchwald, Kasriel Kastel, Zalman Kastel, Ben Tzion Krasnianski, Shlomo Kugel, Joe Schwartz and countless others.

I am also tremendously grateful for the many friends and colleagues who stood by me and encouraged me as I was developing my stand-up comedy act at the Improv, Catch a Rising Star and The Comedy Store, especially Chris Albrecht, Budd Friedman, Gilbert Gottfried, Larry David, Jaime Klein, Jay Leno, Rick Newman, Cary Odes, Garry Shandling, Mitzi Shore and many others.

Finally, overcoming the technical aspects of bringing this book from manuscript to print would not have been possible without the invaluable publishing guidance of Zalman Goldstein of The Jewish Learning Group.

To everyone else who helped make this possible, thank you!

–Richard

Dedications

In memory of Ronnie and Marjorie

ଏଠ ଔ

Dedicated to Joni

Preface

This book is about the path I started, many years ago now, looking for a way back to my Judaism.

I want my story, just one person's story, to be very much an impetus, a catalyst, an enabler, a source of surety and confidence to anyone who would like to learn more about the possibilities of returning to and furthering his or her Judaism. The decision I hope each Jewish person will make for herself or himself will be to accept an invitation; an invitation to travel. In fact, whether we know it or not, our bags have been packed for years, and when we become ready, we leave the luggage we don't need behind. On this new journey, old baggage is nothing more than—old baggage. What we will want to take with us, though, is not the baggage of old, but the treasures of old. It's our own decision, within our own timeline, and at our own pace. I hope you will agree, after reading this book, it's something to think about.

CHAPTER ONE

Alaska the Beautiful

I'm on a plane flying out of Los Angeles with two other comedians from the Comedy Store—David Strassman, a tall, Ivy League-type from the Midwest and Larry Miller, a balding, slightly stocky friend from the showcase comedy clubs in New York. I had been asked to fill in for a fellow comedian, a friend and co-writer I had been working with at that time, Howie Mandel, when he couldn't make the booking. It was 1981. We were scheduled to do a long four-day weekend of shows at a nightclub in Anchorage, Alaska called PJ's.

We were pumped! Alaska! Tundra! Glaciers! Eskimos!

The plane took off full from Los Angeles, and after the first stop in Seattle the plane emptied out, so that when we took off again it was just the three of us and the flight staff. We each had our own bevy of flight attendants, one for each beverage. The on-the-road, comedy-club lifestyle. A life of distractions. We drank those little airplane bottles of liquor until we had what seemed to be about ten bowling lanes of bottle pins set up. Mush! We, of course, swore after that flight—except for any showbiz-obligated moments—that we would never drink again.

Anchorage. Freezing cold. Snow on the ground. It was early November. Living in southern California, we had each brought all the spring jackets we owned to wear. It was like being banished to Bogie-land. The sun came out in the morning to take a look, and would quickly say *uh uh*, and turn the other way. But we were excited. We were in Alaska! Fresh, clean air. No Los Angeles smog. Panoramic views of snow-capped mountains we could reach out and outline. A real respite from L.A.

℘ ℭ

The first show for the comics was at ten o'clock that night. At about two in the afternoon, we went from our condominium apartment to the club, about two blocks away. Condominium apartments are owned by comedy clubs to house the show's comics for that week. A lot cheaper than renting motel rooms every time. And sometimes nicer.

Except for the refrigerators. The refrigerators were always stocked with what we assumed was the previous week's comics' food: white bread, cereal, bologna, mustard, milk.... Sounds reasonable, but there was absolutely no way of knowing if the food was left over from the comics from the previous week—or from vaudeville...! Or if it was even left over by comics at all. We wouldn't dare touch it. We figured that if the housekeeper was afraid to touch it—and she's a professional—we wouldn't stand a chance!

ℒ ℛ

It took us all of the first day to realize that this was not a comedy club at all. This club only brought in comics from Los Angeles on the weekends to elevate their reputation. We were actually the ones brought in to add class to the place. *Us!*

When we had arrived in the afternoon, one of the owners, an ex-con type (what am I saying, ex-con, he looked like he was a current con on a work-release program) greeted us. This greeting was more like a frisk. And when he was assured we weren't carrying any weapons, or even knew how or why or where to buy any weapons, he asked us to step up to the bar for a *hello* drink. Sure, why not. We swore we would never drink again, but, you know, this could count for one of those showbiz-obligated moments. It was 2:30 in the afternoon. He lined up the shots. I can assure you, the familiar toast of *l'chaim* was nowhere to be heard. One shot glass filled with whatever it was filled with and we were smashed! He set up another line of shots. And then another. And then another.... Downing these shots moved very quickly from a show-business obligation to out-and-out liver abuse! We were literally dragged back to our condo, and fell fast asleep on any piece of furniture or floor that was in front of us. If it had been Purim, it would have been a joy. But I can assure you, it wasn't a joy. No one in this place had an inkling of what Purim was except Larry and me.

We woke up in the evening, went back to the club, and saw the audience lined up outside for—at last—the comedy show. (It was mostly students from the university.) They threw a microphone stand on stage—and it was a comedy club. The current ex-convict-owner was conveniently the Master of Ceremonies too. Training for this job, I assumed, he did not have... He grabbed the microphone, gazed out at the crowd, moved his head from side to side—in a manner that made sure nobody would ever think about laughing—and then he spoke. "Ladies and gentlemens," he slinked. "Listen up 'cause we're gonna have a comedy show now!" This guy made Rocky Balboa sound like Sir Laurence Olivier.

He jumped off the stage, stood at the side of the room, folded his arms very slowly, and stared at the audience with one of those *go on, give me an excuse* looks. With each joke or routine, the audience didn't know whether to laugh or write out their wills. It was chilling.

Finally, when it was my turn during the evening to be introduced, (the audience being very well behaved) he leaped up onto the stage again and shouted into the microphone: "You's better pipe down for this guy also or we're gonna throw you's all outta here, cover charges or no cover charges! Here's anudder guy dat we brought here from Los Angeles—Ricky Norris!"

And I'm thinking, *Thank G-d he doesn't know my name!*

While I'm on stage, the current convict/emcee, now the bouncer, is walking from table to table, bending over into the middle of each, and threatening each person to either zip-up-the-lip or get dragged outta there! I got the distinct feeling that dragging people around was a mainstay of this club's ownership-and-Master-of-Ceremonies "training."

I did my act as fast as I could, and got off stage as fast as I could.

℘ ℭ

On the plane back to Los Angeles I looked out over the Pacific Ocean. The flight attendant came by and asked if I'd like a beverage. I looked at her differently than I had on the trip up to Alaska. I told her what soda I wanted, and thanked her. I thought about the men and women, some pitiful, who frequented that club in Anchorage, not only on nights when there was no comedy show, but in the afternoons as well. The people who worked there, the people who drank there. Their lives brought them to Alaska, but their circumstances brought them to that bar—a place as cold as they were. I felt so sorry for them and the dead end they were at. And they all must've felt equally as sorry for us comedians, performing in such a place.

They were stuck in Alaska doing whatever they did, and I was stuck on the road doing what I did. But the dead-end streets I had been attracted to in comedy clubs would not be so attractive to me anymore. I thought about possibilities of other avenues ... and venues. Which ones, who knew. How to find those avenues? Who knew. How to continue with my work, and how to ever build my career, for me, in those dead-end clubs—even the most upstanding ones—who knew. How could I guarantee that I wouldn't be vulnerable to the same temptations on the road as I'd always been? Who knew. It was all personal. How others dealt with the road and show business was their business. How I dealt with it was mine. It is said "You can't go home again." Maybe so. But certainly you can remember, and certainly you can begin to build something new—again.

Lessons from Alaska the beautiful.

CHAPTER TWO

Building ...
A House of Cards

I became a working actor in New York in 1972. And after several years acting in plays, musicals, touring companies, and summer theater, I started building my stand-up comedy act and worked as a stand-up comedian at the two main comedy clubs in New York at that time: the Improv and Catch A Rising Star.

After working all over the country, and Canada—two shows Friday, two shows Saturday, and shows every other day that came with a night—I made it to national network television.

In that same year, 1981, I got a guest spot on *The Merv Griffin Show*—a highly rated evening talk show that gave new comedians a chance to show what they could do. I showed them what I could do, and after my first appearance I was invited back to do the show from The Riviera Hotel in Las Vegas. I was on my way—both to Las Vegas and to a promising career.

Soon after, my agent at the William Morris Agency submitted sketches I had written to (at that time) SCTV (*Second City Television*, in Canada). Barry Sand, the producer of *Second City*, took my material to a new show in New York for which he was going to be the producer, NBC's *Late Night with David Letterman*. I was hired as a writer for the show, and I was on my way again—back to New York.

One of my favorite ideas that I submitted for the show was to select two people in the audience to go on a "date in the Green Room." It would be set up as a tiny nightclub—featuring a lounge singer—as the couple would get to know each other over dinner. Dave would interrupt the couple in segments throughout the show, culminating in the two being "married" by the show's announcer or one of the show's tech crew.

I had a great time as a writer on the show. But nobody on staff at *Late Night* was from the stand-up comedy world—except David Letterman and his head writer. They had both been stand-up comedians at The Comedy Store. When my option as a writer came up, I was asked to be a guest on the show as a comedian. In the corporate world this would be known as being *kicked upstairs*: middle management is not your cup of tea, so we're making you a ... vice president!

I would gladly have stayed on as a writer if I could, but I was thrilled to be a guest on the show and also thrilled that I wouldn't have to give any more of my ideas or material to anybody else! All my thinking and all my writing was focused back to my stand-up act. As it happened, if I wanted to move on to another television writing job, David Letterman was nice enough to write a recommendation letter for me. In the letter he wrote, he said: "... Richard would be a valuable addition to any writing staff." But I wanted to continue with my stand-up act. And so I prepared for my first guest appearance on *Late Night with David Letterman*.

℘ ℭ

The material I did on the show seemed to be less of a concern to me than what I would wear. I had been working on my material for several years at the clubs in New York, and was pretty much certain of the material. But what should I wear? I didn't have a clue. (This was the same dilemma I had faced before doing the *Merv Griffin Show* and then the *Mike Douglas Show*.) After struggling with it from the time I knew I'd be on the show until the night before, I finally decided on an outfit—I wore a shirt and a pair of pants. A clear fashion statement to America that I haven't the slightest idea what to wear.

The material I would choose to do for the show (and for other TV appearances after that) was from my act in the clubs. There was:

Why do they call dead people late? They're not late; they're not coming! They're not out for coffee, they're not stuck in traffic, they're just not gonna be there. Is this guy coming or what? It's been about two years now. I think we can eat.

And: I recently had a change of address. I didn't move; I just changed my address. It's working out great! I haven't paid a bill in six months. I don't think they know where I am.

And: Who wrote that "Days of the Months" poem? Thirty days has September, April, June, and November, all the rest have thirty-one ... except February which has twenty-eight days and on a leap year it has twenty-nine days and ... I don't want to be a poet anymore!

And: I went on a tour of Ford's Theatre in Washington, DC. That's where President Abraham Lincoln was assassinated. They showed us the balcony where President Lincoln was shot. It's all roped off; nobody can sit there. I think it's incredible; after all these years, it's still not safe.

And: There's a dish on every Chinese menu in every Chinese restaurant called *Happy Family*. I find it very disconcerting how beef, chicken, snow peas, and lychees can get along better than my actual family.

℘ ℭ

I became a frequent guest on the show. I was called over to sit at the desk with David after my monologue, and we talked about the material we had prepared to talk about at the desk. I brought out pictures of my recent trip to England, the highlight being a picture of the Queen's plumber's van paying a visit to Buckingham Palace. (This interested me greatly, and so it became material to talk about with David.)

One memorable night on the show, I must mention, was when I had been scheduled to do a guest spot, and was *bumped* (moved to another night) because the comedian Albert Brooks was on the show that night also. He sat at the desk with David and it went a bit too long so I was told they would have me back another night, which they did. I didn't give it a second thought—I was in the same studio and supposed to be on the same show as Albert Brooks! To anyone who knows comedy, he is, in my opinion, and in many others', the most innovative and funny comedian there ever was. A highlight of any comedian's career has to be being bumped by Albert Brooks!

℘ ℭ

Most comedians, given the chance to be a guest on *Late Night* or *The Tonight Show*, were obliged to choose one show or the other. The shows were competitive when it came to comedians. The comedy clubs in N.Y. and L.A. were also like this. If you worked at the Improv, you most likely couldn't work at the Comedy Store.

There were exceptions though. Budd Friedman, the owner of the Improv, liked my stand-up from my days at the New York Improv. Mitzi Shore, the owner of the Comedy Store, also liked my work. I was lucky—I could work both clubs. And the choice for television at that time was made for me already: I would appear on *Late Night with David Letterman*.

Back in New York, after my first appearance on *Late Night with David Letterman*, I became a frequent, periodic guest on the show. From there, I went on to headline most of the nation's top comedy clubs and open for numerous star attractions at that time, such as: Air Supply, Little River Band, Warren Zevon, and many others. Most of the arena venues were huge! The comedy clubs held one hundred, two hundred people or so—and all of a sudden I was working in arenas that sat three thousand, five thousand, and even ten thousand people!

I did the same act I did at the clubs—only louder!

Among the venues I worked were Westbury Music Fair, Resorts International in Atlantic City, Merriweather-Post Pavilion, Warwick Musical Theatre, and Canada's Wonderland.

My first arena venue was Westbury Music Fair, in Westbury, Long Island—a theater-in-the-round where the stage moved very slowly around the 360-degree audience. I had never worked on a stage that moved. And I had never worked in front of that many people—about three thousand. I was petrified. They gave me the five-minute warn-ing to be ready to go on stage, and I walked to the entrance of the backstage area, a long tunnel that I assumed led to the stage. It did. As I started walking, I looked behind me and saw a huge man in a suit with his hands clasped in front of him, staring straight ahead. No *hello*, no *good luck*, no nothing. He just followed me into the tunnel. I immediately felt a kindred spirit with anyone on Death Row. I reached a door at the end of the tunnel, heard my name over the speaker system, and the huge man opened the door.

He literally pushed me forward onto the stage. The audience was applauding politely, and I started running around the stage trying to find the microphone. The problem was that the equipment of the headline act, the Little River Band, was already set on stage. It looked like an electronics fair. I was afraid to touch anything for fear I would be electrocuted. And I was afraid to touch anything because I didn't know how the big man backstage would feel about it. I assumed he would not like it. So I kept darting in and out of the equipment until I saw a microphone on a stand apart from the guitars and piano and the speakers. I grabbed the microphone and blew into it. A loud gust of air resonated all over the theater. Even *I* got scared. I said, "There, I've just blown into each of your ears. I feel so much closer to you now."

It got a laugh, and even applause. I took the microphone off the stand, started running around the stage—in and out and over the wires and equipment—and started pretty much screaming my act; the same act I had done the night before, and countless times through the years, at the showcase comedy clubs in Manhattan.

I had hit the big time. These were great venues. Very classy. Great money. And great fun. After a while I realized that the big man leading me down the corridor to the stage was there so that I didn't have second thoughts of turning around and leaving the building. Once I entered that tunnel, it was reach the stage on my own power or reach the stage being carried there by this giant! I chose my own power every time.

₭ ℒ

I would go on the road, come back to New York, open my mail, do a guest appearance on *Late Night with David Letterman*, maybe open for a star attraction or two, and then go back out on the road. I was riding a whirlwind. Audiences loved what I was doing, the club owners loved what I was doing, and the money was rolling in—and rolling out just as fast.

I didn't like my road act anywhere near as much as I liked my act that I had been working on in New York. The audiences in New York were more discerning, and I brought material to the New York venues that I hoped lived up to those expectations. I worked harder to write more clever, quality material, which New York audiences demanded and appreciated. And I knew the New York club owners and other comedians were watching. On the road, no one from the industry was watching. And the arena audiences, listening to a twenty-minute set before a star attraction, demanded less. I could only use the most accessible material. Nothing edgy. And sometimes *too clever* would go over the heads of that type of audience. Sometimes the bands I opened for would attract much younger crowds.

I found myself not having the constriction of having to write material for a late-night talk show anymore—but now I was controlled by the larger venues, and wasting the freedom I was given at the comedy clubs on the road. Instead of keeping the quality of my material up to my own taste and standards—material that got me the job on *Late Night with David Letterman* to begin with—I was appeasing audiences on the road. I performed my act to their taste, not to what I knew to be mine. They loved it. I hated it.

However, I *was* having a great time. In fact, I found myself focusing mostly on the good times I was having—not on my work. The great time I was having made me lose sight of a larger goal—and it really took me away from thinking about any goal at all. And though it may sound completely implausible—it seemed the more I strayed from what I knew were my real capabilities—the more work I got! And, after a while, my act didn't look like the same act I had earned my good reputation with at the important industry showcase clubs for comedians in N.Y. and L.A.

I started getting accustomed to the road for the lack of responsibility it required and afforded me. It was like an ongoing working vacation. I became somewhat addicted to the fun.

Sorry to break the show-business myth here, but with me, and I'm sure with many, many others, there was no substance abuse, no heavy drinking all the time, no partying all the time.... Oh, sorry. Except for the last one, now that I think of it ... *that* wasn't a myth.

For me the fun came first, the work came second ... and the goals came last. It wasn't substance abuse—it was fun abuse.

On Monday mornings, after a week at a comedy club or a few arenas, I would fly back to New York, go to the comedy clubs, and then fly out again on Tuesdays to begin a new string of week-long bookings.

Tuesday nights were usually dollar-beer nights at many of the comedy clubs. Perfect! Less pressure, less expectations. And

Wednesday nights were Ladies Nights.... Am I beginning to get my point across here? I was in heaven ... in that other place commonly thought of as just below heaven!

Everyone was happy with my act on stage: the majority of the audiences were happy, those club owners were happy; everyone was happy! Apparently I wasn't really there—so I couldn't tell you if I was happy or not. The same person who had cared so much about what would be considered quality material and maintaining the high standard he knew he was capable of achieving wasn't really there.

But Where Was I?

I was hiding. I was hiding the real me so that the real me wouldn't get emotionally hurt. That's where I was. And if I would only have continued working on my act in New York for a few more years, I would have developed that original act I knew I had inside of me—and that would have given me the security that would likely have carried me—through the years—to all the venues, with an act that would have better represented me. Audiences showing their approval for *that*, to me, would have meant everything.

But I opted to *fit in* rather than to *stand out*. It was nothing new to me. It felt almost comfortable, secure—not being myself. I used it as a cover throughout my childhood and my youth and into my adult life. I couldn't be hurt—if I wasn't being my real self.

But presenting someone other than my real persona on stage meant I had to re-create that *someone* night after night on stage. It was exhausting. I began to dread going on stage. And what made it even more damaging to me was the fact that I never stopped working. For many years. I couldn't—I was too successful.

Along with achievement, wealth, fame, rank—which, in reality, I only knew a bit of each—one of the definitions of success is *a favorable or satisfactory outcome or result.* That would have to wait for the future. It would have to wait because as much as I continued trying, I couldn't find the center in my stand-up act, like the famous *through-line* in acting, that point that I could rely on every night, to find my stage character, to lift me and carry me through each show with the same persona and energy and delivery vital in re-creating the same performances. So instead of continuing to look for my real self, my real confidence and conviction—my same true character on stage each night—the eventual frustration led me to go looking for it elsewhere.

I couldn't avoid it any longer. The center I couldn't find in my stand-up—whether I made that conscious decision or not—was not on stage, but in my life.

CHAPTER THREE

And So, I Needed to Look at My Life

I grew up being vilified in my own family. It made me an outsider.

I was the youngest of two by six years, always wanting nothing more than to *fit in*, to be part of my own family. But I wasn't. There was them—and then there was me. Mostly ignored by my brother throughout my childhood and teen years; berated at any given chance by my mother; and having a nondescript relationship with my father. In my childhood and youth, I can't remember ever having a conversation with my father or my brother. It seemed they just weren't available, or interested. And any conversations I had with my mother mostly subjugated me.

Today, as an adult, I'm 5' 9½" and weigh about 150 pounds. When I was growing up, my heaviest weight (when I got to college) was 230 pounds. In my home, I was never allowed to forget that I was fat. And it's the image I have of myself to this day.

My parents and brother were business people. Office people. Mostly serious people. I wanted to be funny. You'd think that would be an asset in a house like that. In-house entertainment. A perfect match! It wasn't. It was the boy's-side story of the Cinderella story.

In many ways I felt I had no secure home base. Physically, yes. Emotionally, no. And, as I've learned since, a part of our obligation to honor our parents is forgiving and appreciating the sacrifices they made in order to give their children the creature comforts children need.

It's hard to be a parent. And my parents had the additional hardship of coming to a new country, not out of choice, but to escape the horrors and dangers of state-sanctioned anti-semitism. We can't imagine their plight. And we can't begin to analyze their actions. They were forced to bring their fears and confusion to America. And they had to sort it out as they moved along. And for the most part, I'm sure unwittingly, the children bore the brunt of it. Even though my parents, thank G-d, were not caught up in the oncoming Holocaust then, all Jews are Holocaust survivors. All. What allowed our people to pick up the pieces was the fact that we are a people.

I can honor my parents' memory now, but as I was growing up I only had pent-up rage.

Such fortune we generations of Jews enjoyed by being born in America. We had everything, and have everything. But it came at a cost. We had to bear the emotional hardships, the scars, of the generations before us, to continue on as the generations after. We can always pretend that everything's okay, but only pretend. In reality, we're part of the people to which we are born. And it's up to us to see to it that the next generation looks at Judaism as something strong and lasting. Our roots run deep.

℘ ℭ

Of course, in the comparatively trivial pursuits of the things of our generations, in my particular work I wanted to channel the rage I had into my stand-up act—and I did touch upon it when I first started developing my act in New York, but when I left the showcase comedy clubs (what we looked at as *comedy gymnasiums*) to work on the road, I opted for doing well on stage with material that was getting laughs, material that was working. But, again, not necessarily material that I believed in. In the sport of diving, I was scoring high with the easy jack-knife dive, but trying nothing more difficult than that. I wasn't scoring rage points; I was just scoring points. And for that, I didn't have to keep score.

Rage, to a comedian, is like a power boost. It's like pulling the cord on an outboard motor. Tell a few jokes, do a few middle-of-the-road, easy-to-grasp bits, and then pull the cord ... vroom vroom: rage! Nothing's funnier. On the road, I packed everything else but that. On the road, I couldn't find a reason to perform.

Entertaining audiences was certainly a reason. But I needed something more. I needed to feel as though I was accomplishing something more with my work than just entertainment. I did find the rage *sometimes*, and it was very funny, and made me feel great, because I was getting laughs being the real me, but I couldn't replicate it night after night. It was my greatest flaw in being a stand-up comedian: I was inconsistent. And so I kept the rage inside, hoping it would come out in my act by chance. And sometimes it did. And sometimes there were standing ovations. But I couldn't consistently guarantee it.

The silent angst I carried around with me tainted everything I did and everyone I knew. Everyone. And soon it became more frustration than rage. When I gave into it, I lashed out at people, at situations—at anything. When you want to throw stones—figuratively speaking—at someone or something, you have to stop, pick up the stones, and then throw the stones. You may hit the intended target, or not. Either way, all you've done for certain is alienate another person and, probably more damaging, stopped yourself from moving forward.

I knew I had to somehow address my rage, but I also knew that I had to do it by first putting down the stones.

I started out with such high ideals. But now I felt I didn't deserve the success I was facing. I fought that success at every juncture. It seemed like the dial on the compass wasn't pointing anywhere anymore. In fact, the compass was gone. Lost.

What do you do if you lose something? Retrace your steps. Who was the person I started as? Well, I've always been funny. I was being funny, and making money at it. But I had to get back to something inside me that was more indicative of who I was. Like stripping away layers to reveal the core. Unfortunately, I didn't know how to do that. Who does? But I was ready. I strayed from my goals, my standards—myself. And one sure way of beginning to heal is to realize and face the fact that healing is needed.

CHAPTER FOUR

Prospecting

Throughout my life, I'd always been concerned with having a good time rather than spending time nurturing my spiritual side.

Having a good time, to me, *was* my spiritual side. What's more spiritual than having fun? But I distinctly remember thinking when I was in my twenties that as a Jewish person, I wanted to do something more Jewish—but I didn't really know how to do that. And, yes, I didn't give it any priority other than that. At the time, I wasn't affiliated with any synagogue, and I just didn't have the wherewithal to find one on my own, even if it was as easy as knocking on the door of one of the synagogues I knew existed in the area. I would never stop to go inside. If there was a comedy show or a dance club or a music club to go into, I would make it my business to find it, get there, go inside with my friends and have some fun! But a synagogue? A thousand excuses: I don't remember where it is; what do I wear? Do I need a ticket? Maybe they started already; maybe I'll miss some fun that my friends are having without me; maybe I'll go next week....

I didn't exactly go knocking on any synagogue door or even look up a list of synagogues in my neighborhood, but at the right time, I did find out how to connect with my Judaism—and even though it was the very last thing I would ever have expected—I slowly became observant. And before you think, "Observant? Woah!—Bye bye, I'm outta here," please read on....

&) CR

Many observant Jews have one foot in the secular world and one foot in the Jewish world. A rabbi with whom I once studied, and whose synagogue I attend frequently, said of me that I have two feet in the secular world and two feet in the Jewish world. In my practice of Judaism, I label myself observant, meaning I observe the laws of the Torah as best I can. I considered my family's household traditionally Jewish. But one important fact that made all the difference was that we were kosher (in the house). But on the whole, we couldn't be called observant. I learned about true observance later on. And incorporating that observance into my life, on the whole, made all the difference.

&) CR

My practice of the rituals of Judaism and my daily prayers serve me well. I've learned what to do and how to perform what's known as the *mitzvahs* (mitzvahs being not merely good deeds, but connections to G-d— like keeping kosher). And I've found that an unaffiliated Jew might be more observant, in ways, than any given Orthodox Jew. Externally we have no idea how any given Jew adheres to his or her Judaism, or how spiritually elevated that person might be. And nobody has the right to question or look down on another Jew for how they might or might not practice their Judaism. Any non-practicing Jewish person might simply not yet be in possession of the information that might very much interest them. Labels are just labels. Before deciding what's inside, it's always best to read the ingredients.... And I always think: to get a picture of what's really inside a person, it's best to focus on the person—not on their real or perceived status in life.

℘ ℩

Being connected to something gives a person a purpose. And while we're connected to a lot of things in our lives that give us purpose, being born Jewish gives us that deeper connection, that deeper purpose, already. Is it worth exploring? Well, when a boxer who prays before a fight is asked if his prayers help, he answers, "Not if you can't fight."

But if you can fight, then determination, belief in something, purpose, and connection just might mean the difference between winning and losing.

℘ ℩

To most, religion is too much trouble to stick to on a daily basis. There's always a more important distraction. But if life is sometimes called a game, religion would be like musical chairs. While the music's playing, everything's fine. But when the music stops, everyone scrambles to find a chair. Being religious is like carrying around something like that chair, a place of comfort and connection, all the time. How comfortably we carry it around, and how often we use it also makes quite a difference.

ↄ Ↄ

Almost everyone is accustomed to only looking at religion on the serious side. And the image and practice of religion is serious. Somber. Introspective. And sometimes extremely tedious. But as in stage lighting for a play, religion is meant to illuminate our lives—so that we can live our lives. In *Hamlet*, Shakespeare wrote, *The play's the thing*. He didn't say, *The lighting's the thing*. Very few people walk out at the end of a play talking about the lighting! But if there was, indeed, no lighting—that's all they would talk about.

ↄ Ↄ

Belief in a religion affords structure. It's a *social contract*—made with oneself and with G-d and with a community. Yes, a very serious matter. But you can be religious no matter what your religion, and still be not so serious.

To Jews, laughing about ourselves has always kept us sane—in an all-too-often insane world. Unfortunately, religious Jews—Orthodox Jews—are not usually counted in that number of frequent laughers. But it's about time they put this into their learning regiment: learning how to laugh. Tears and laughter are interconnected. If we cry long enough, we'll laugh. And if we laugh long enough, we'll cry. We shouldn't be afraid to laugh! Believe me, I've heard of more people being bored to tears than, thank G-d, dying of laughter. There's some middle ground there for sure. We just have to find it. And I think it's worth looking for.

 ℘ ℭ

I actually found being observant less challenging than being non-observant. Being non-observant means focusing on everything out there. Being observant means focusing on everything out there and also everything within. When I was able to do that I was able to realize what was getting in the way; what was preventing me from moving forward. Having the ability and wherewithal to peel away the layers inside unfolds the layers outside. Like the classic example in archery: many serious people pull the string on the bow back, but never seem to let go. I learned to pull the string back, and was fortunate enough to allow myself to, indeed, let go. New goals are always out there, and I still manage to keep hitting new ones by learning to remove the layers that cover up the ability (that exists in each of us) to simply let go.

CHAPTER FIVE

The Old Neighborhoods

The person you invariably become is modeled, of course, in very many ways after the experiences and images of your past. In the neighborhood where I grew up in the Bronx, an elderly, energetic man would show up once a week, late in the afternoon, in the court-yards of the apartment houses that lined out streets. He would look up at the row of five-story buildings and shout at the top of his lungs, "High-cash clothes! High-cash clothes!" He was like the ice cream man of *shmatas* (ragged old clothing/dry goods).

I couldn't understand what he was doing; was he buying clothes or selling clothes, or just shouting? If he was selling clothes, why would anyone want to pay *high cash* for, what I assumed was, old clothing? Shouldn't old clothing be cheap? Wouldn't he have been better off yelling, "Cheap old clothes"?

And if he was buying old clothing for high cash—why weren't thousands of people lining up to bring him their old clothes? Well, they weren't lining up to bring him their old clothes because the term *high cash* to him and the term high cash to somebody who actually knew what the term meant were two different things.

He would go from courtyard to courtyard screaming for someone to offer him a piece of clothing he could buy for the lowest possible price imaginable, so he could, of course, sell it for the highest possible price imaginable. Nobody would go near him, but he kept on shouting and shouting, "High-cash clothes! High-cash clothes!" You could hear him in New Rochelle!

We listened to his shouts, kept the windows closed, and waited for him to ... shut up. He never did. Eventually we just learned to live with the sound of the high-cash clothes man. It was a part of living in the Bronx (and, come to think of it, New Rochelle, too); that was part of its charm.

$$\text{\Large ℘ ☙}$$

I remember thinking, What a thing to be: a high-cash clothes salesman. And, of course, I would think about what I was going to be when I grew up. And in my little-boy wisdom, I somehow knew that the high-cash clothing business was not going to show up high on my prospective career list.

But it got me to thinking, years later, about the Bronx, about that high-cash clothes man—and about what a person becomes.

I followed my instincts and chose not to be a high-cash clothing salesman. My college offered no classes in it. Go figure. But my college did have a great theater department. I acted in many of the plays, and that stayed with me.

Do you become what you do? For many people, possibly. I've got to go back to the Bronx to find out if that high-cash clothes man is still there. I don't think he is. The buildings are taller now. They only built buildings five stories tall then because if one more floor was added the landlord would have had to install an elevator. Hmm ... the Bronx. Hmm ... magic.

$\wp$ $\wr$

I hadn't been back to the Bronx for many years. But wherever I go, I can tell you, the lovable Bronx goes with me—as I'm sure it does for so many others. It's such an indelible image; like an internal tattoo.

Years later, when I would travel to the red-neck nooks and crannies of places like east and west Texas, I would sometimes stand motionless, taken aback by how foreign the towns and the Texans' ways were to me. I had no perspective on Texas whatsoever, other than the old Western movies. A nice Jewish boy from the Bronx—in cowboy country. *Podna!*

I would think back to my boyhood on Burnside Avenue, close my eyes, and try to somehow put the *hamishe* (simple, home-style) aromas of the old Eastern European-style kosher bakeries (the most famous: Garden Bakery and G&R Bakery) and the Mosholu Parkway, Jerome Avenue aromas of Schweller's Delicatessen—alongside the sweet, smoky smells of a mesquite-coal, Lubbock-type barbecue. Oy. Culture shock! The two smells coming together would have been nice—for culture-exchange sake—but, yet, apart they would stay. Apparently *potato latkes* and anything mesquite barbecued in an earthen pit—in any part of Texas—was a *shidduch* (match) for which the Lone Star State and Schweller's Delicatessen was not quite ready! And neither was Burnside Avenue. And, I'm not sure, but I think there might be a distinct *Latkes Prohibition Law* still on the books in Texas that dates back to the day Davy Crockett first asked, "So what size do these coonskin caps come in?"

When I found myself in places like North Dakota, I would think back to the throngs of people in the Bronx, all dressed up (*far-put-sed*, as my mother would say) on the High Holy Days on the Grand Concourse.... In North Dakota-speak it would be sort of like the Easter Parade—without the bunnies.

I traveled all over, carrying the memories of growing up Jewish in the Bronx with me wherever I went. My parents and my grandparents also traveled, but they carried different memories with them. And, as we all must acknowledge, traveling under the harshest of circumstances, from Lida in White Russia and from Yekatrinislav in Ukraine—to America—to the Lower East Side of New York.... A very familiar story to Jews (and to many other groups of people as well). A very familiar place to the huddled masses yearning to breathe free.

₲ ℓ

In those early days, many Jews would work six days a week, Sunday through Friday. They would work through Friday afternoon and then have to quit because they refused to work on Saturday (the Sabbath) and therefore weren't allowed to come back to work on Monday. So then they would have to look for a new job every Sunday.

When I heard of these circumstances for the first time, I grimaced. I couldn't believe it. People had such conviction in their beliefs that they would quit a job after finishing work on Fridays to avoid working Friday nights and Saturdays? Hmm. That's guts! It made an impression on me. I could never imagine doing that.

ℰℛ

From the Lower East Side's overcrowded tenements, couples would marry and move to the country: the Bronx. By the time I arrived on the scene, it wasn't the country anymore. It was the city; close together, but rich with character, and characters! These were less crowded tenement buildings and streets than on the Lower East Side, but they had something the Lower East Side didn't have: huge, green parks! The generation of Jewish immigrants that were able to come to America at that time could now see a brighter, greener, more livable way of life for them and their children.

Images About the Way it Was

There were exquisite movie palaces. Nothing less than exquisite. And nothing less than a palace—showing only one feature movie in that one theater! The flagship movie house in the Bronx, and possibly the nation, was Loew's Paradise: glorious statues in the lobby; panoramic sky views of twinkling stars on the immense ceiling inside the sprawling theater. And a giant goldfish pond in the lobby—with giant live goldfish. If you put a giant live goldfish pond in a movie theater now, people would bring fishing tackle!

The Bronx (and Brooklyn) had huge cafeterias where people would sit all day long—and sometimes even buy something! They were like adult lunch rooms. The people would eat a little, and sit a lot. How people got so fat was a gastronomical wonder that still baffles nutritionists to this day. One can only assume that these people never stopped eating when they got home.

And the candy stores. Oh, the candy stores. A small soda fountain glass of Coca Cola: five cents.... And the egg creams.... Ooh, the egg creams. It would take a separate book. If you don't know how to make an egg cream, or don't know what an egg cream is—let us pray.

ⅎ ℳ

Those were the images, those were the times, those were our lives. The Bronx Jewish culture. The candy stores devolved into what later became known as *delis*. During the period I was describing, delis were always short for delicatessens; and mostly kosher delicatessens, like Schwellers: a sit-down restaurant that served corned beef, salami, brisket, turkey and pastrami on rye bread as a club or as an open-faced sandwich on a plate drenched in gravy. Those were delis! A deli disguised as a grocery store is not a deli. It's a grocery store. The *delis*—delicatessens—are still around, but there are not so many.

The candy stores personified the past I left. To Jews it was our everyday culture, it seemed, and now *a candy store no more*; our meeting place, our hangout, our lunch place, a social hall for the young and old, faded. For many of us these parts of the Jewish Bronx were our identities. We seemed to exist because these places existed—these temporary places. And as thousands of people moved away, the Bronx continued on, but in another form. The old Bronx was magic—we thought it would last.

CHAPTER SIX

Passover:
A Deal's a Deal

On the door to the lobby of the apartment building where I grew up there was a large *mezuzah* containing ancient Hebrew writing that, I was certain, was put there by our landlord in ancient Hebrew times.

On the door to *our* apartment we had our own mezuzah as well; but it was anybody's guess what the markings on the scroll inside that mezuzah looked like because checking a mezuzah meant periodically sending it to a trained scribe, who would carefully look at each letter on the mezuzah's scroll before approving it. We weren't so fancy. To us, checking the mezuzah meant staring at it and saying, "Yep, that's a mezuzah alright!"

While all things Jewish always interested me, I never really delved into it wholeheartedly, partly because nothing about it seemed reachable: the New Year was in September; you could get seriously hurt when rocking back and forth while praying; eating a cheeseburger wasn't a good thing.... (Oh, cheese you could eat—and then sometime in the near future, a burger—but not at the same time.) And even with all these rules, I never gave up on Jewish logic. Not because I ever saw any logic in it at first, but because I just couldn't wait to find out, at some point, what the possible logic behind the whole thing could be! And I will never stop hoping that the prohibition on eating a cheeseburger is—please G-d—a typographical error!

I, of course, tried asking my parents questions about Judaism, but every question I asked would get me the same answer from one parent or the other: "We're not so religious."

I tell you, asking questions about religion in my house was like someone asking for yogurt in the 1950s! I would get one of those "You know, this boy of ours might not be so normal" looks. (Implying that in my house if you tried to be too religious or too healthy, you must have a problem.) But despite being not-so-religious (and, I'm guessing, not so healthy by today's standards), we were very Jewish. Well, very Jewish, yes, but when it came to Jewish prayer and ritual, atheists could have given us some helpful tips! The only thing I can say is that if there are a thousand Jewish things you're supposed to be doing (and, believe me, if you're Jewish, there *are* a thousand Jewish things you're supposed to be doing), and you do three of them, those three things are probably so odd and so complicated that you don't have to do any of the other nine hundred ninety-seven, and you'd still be considered very Jewish!

Taking precedence over all Jewish laws and customs is the popular understanding that you can get away with doing *nothing* Jewish—and still be considered very Jewish—if you repeat the sound *tsk* over and over, very rapidly, in reaction to any catastrophic or, for that matter, insignificant occurrence! What? You forgot to buy ketchup? *Tsk, tsk, tsk, tsk, tsk....* And in the next breath, what? You heard that gravity is in limited supply and we'll be running out of it next Tuesday? *Tsk, tsk, tsk, tsk, tsk.*

As a matter of fact, become a *tsk-er* and you could be the Archbishop of Canterbury, and you'd still be considered very Jewish!

ℰ ℭ

My parents came from Russia via Ellis Island—before it had a Mister Softee concession. They got their papers, got their shots, their names—no custard though—and they were off to the Lower East Side of Manhattan as small children with their respective families to live the new life. A life of new hope and of never-ending dreams—and on the Lower East Side of New York in those years—a life of taking baths in the kitchen!

A bathtub in close proximity to the kitchen table was one of the luxuries of Lower East Side tenement living in the early 1900s—which would prompt anyone to wonder why a generation would strive to better themselves, knowing they'd be giving up the refreshing novelty of being part of a family of twelve trying to eat dinner in the same room with a visiting relative asking someone at the table if they wouldn't mind passing the soap!

My parents met, got married, moved to the Bronx (where I like to imagine the unique idea of putting a bathtub *in the bathroom* got started), had two sons, and spoke Yiddish in our two-bedroom apartment when they didn't want my brother and I to understand what they were talking about. To be quite frank, when they spoke *English* I didn't know what they were talking about....

My grandmother set up our kosher kitchen, thanks to her mother, and thanks to her mother's mother and thanks to her mother's mother—and my mother kept it going, thanks to grandma. And to keep it all a secret from my brother and me, they talked about it in Yiddish. So thanks to my mother and her mother (and all the other mothers I mentioned), a nice semblance of Jewish order was maintained in our house. But the world, and the Bronx, I wasn't so sure about. As the Jewish population of the Bronx moved away, the synagogues, the *shuls* and the temples changed with them. (I'm not sure, but I think the Reform temple next to our house on the Grand Concourse was turned into an indoor Calypso Parrot Jungle.)

Passover

Even though we only went to synagogue on the High Holy Days, and then for only short periods of time, we always celebrated Passover. We had wonderful Seders. Not ritualistically spiritual, just wonderful. We had no patience for the *Haggadah* (sort of the program at a Seder). We looked at the *Haggadah* as though it was a compilation of *War and Peace, A Tale of Two Cities* and James A. Michener's *Hawaii!* These works took too long to read—so why read any of it?

Let me walk you through one of our Seders.

We're at the beginning of the Seder where, believe me, it was the best of times and it was the worst of times!

We start with the Four Questions, the heart of the Passover Seder, asked by the youngest child at the table—me! I would ask the questions and everybody would start buzzing, "Isn't that cute, that's so cute."

Leaving Egypt was cute? Can I get some answers here?

I don't ever remember getting any answers to any of the questions at our Passover Seders. Ever. Apparently the only point here was to hear me, or an occasional young cousin, ask the Four Questions. I'm sure the answers were somewhere in the neighborhood, but I assure you, the answers to these questions would, indeed, pass over *our* house completely. Passover is, of course, the time to pass along and enrich the family's younger generation with their Jewish heritage. But I'm afraid all we were doing at our Seders was passing along our particular family heritage: not knowing how to look up the answers to the Four Questions in the table of contents.

But as I look back, I am glad I didn't get any answers to the Four Questions. If my family's source for answering the Four Questions wasn't the *Haggadah*, the answers they would have conjured up might have set Judaism back to the day right before G-d said to Moses, "I'd like you to go back to Egypt to free the people ... how do you feel about locusts?"

$$\wp \, \backsim$$

My house wasn't unusual. Oh, no. (Well it was unusual, but not for that reason.) Seders at our relatives' houses were just as unusual. If Pharaoh had known that some three thousand years later such casualness would have been taking place in Jewish homes *he* would have been the one to leave Egypt! And the Jewish people would have been known to this day as the ancient people who drove Pharaoh out of Egypt! And the Four Questions to this day would have been: Why did Pharaoh leave Egypt? Weren't *we* the ones who were supposed to go? He was doing so well, where was he thinking of going? And why are we the ones who have to eat matzah if he was the one to leave?

Right before Pharaoh was thinking of leaving Egypt (to straighten things out for posterity) he would have invited Moses to accompany him, man to man, on a rowboat ride up the Nile River, to try one last-ditch effort to stay on as head of Egypt.

After rowing for forty minutes Pharaoh would have brought the oars back inside the boat, gazed up at the stars in the ancient Egyptian sky, looked around to make sure there were no hieroglyphic paparazzi nearby, and said, "Moses, I like it here, I don't want to leave Egypt. So I'll give you one more chance. If I stay—and let your people go—what guarantees can you give me that they won't make a game of all of this in, let's say, the twenty-first century Bronx?"

And Moses would have replied in frustration, "Guarantees? What guarantees can I give you? The only thing I can tell you is that if you free us from being slaves I'll give you my word that my people will have every good intention of traveling to the desert to serve G-d. That's what you agreed to, right? That you would free us so that we could go and serve G-d. You're not reneging on your promise, are you?" And Moses would've added, "But I can only speak for the people you are freeing here today; future generations, I'm afraid, can't be my responsibility."

And Pharaoh quickly would've replied: "But surely future generations would remember the Passover story, of how you came to me and made my life a living —well, you know what I mean—with the hail storms and the frogs and the snakes, won't they?"

"Please don't forget the boils, Pharaoh," Moses would've said. "I thought the boils were very effective: boils coming out of nowhere, I mean, come on—that's genius."

"Yes! The boils, very annoying, yes," Pharaoh would've continued. "Can we get back to the point here? If your people are being freed to go and serve G-d—then that's what they agree to do. They either serve me, or they serve this ... G-d of yours! That's the agreement. And if it makes you feel any better, you've won. Now take your people and go!"

"Okay, tomorrow we'll just gather up our things and leave," Moses would've agreed. "We'll be out of here no later than four or five o'clock."

"In the morning?" Pharaoh would have asked.

"What are you—insane, Pharaoh?" Moses would have suggested. "No, not five in the morning. We're not all farmers, you know. Five in the afternoon!"

"Oh no!" Pharaoh would've blurted. "I want you out of here by eleven!" (This, by the way, is where I believe we get the familiar check-out time used by most motels since the Exodus.)

"Eleven it is. You won't regret this, Pharaoh," Moses would've said kindly. "We'll stick to our pledge. These are a difficult people sometimes, but they know how to honor an agreement. We'll have it written down, I'm sure, so that every year at this time everyone will know what happened in Egypt and how we were slaves to you and how you let us go free so we could become, well, sort of like slaves to G-d.... Hey, why are we always slaves? That's the deal I made? We're still like slaves?"

"Moses!" Pharaoh would've shouted. "I would like to remind you that you and your people would still be slaves in Egypt if your G-d didn't make locusts come out of my ears!"

"And the boils," Moses would've said proudly again. "Please Pharaoh, I beg you, do not forget about the boils!"

"Moses, I've changed my mind again, I want you and your people out of here by sunrise! Not eleven! Sunrise!" Pharaoh would've said. "And

I'm betting even money that your people will forget this whole slave affair as soon as they hit the desert! And as far as future generations go I'm making a side bet that they won't be slaves to G-d at all! Now leave me! And if you think Pharaoh can't see into the future, Moses, he can...! Yul Bryner is going to play me in the movie *The Ten Commandments!*"

"No!" Moses would've surely gasped. "Tell me, who's going to play me?"

"You promise to leave?" Pharaoh would've insisted.

"At first light," Moses would've answered. "I'm telling you, we'll leave so fast that the dough we slap onto that fire won't even have time to even resemble bread! It'll be more like flat, tasteless crackers."

"Very well. Charlton Heston will play you," Pharaoh would've casted.

"Yes!" Moses would've exclaimed. "You can take my staff away from me when you pry it from my cold, dead hands!"

℘ ℭ

When Moses came to his senses again, he would've feared that he might've bamboozled Pharaoh into letting the people go under the guise of serving G-d in the desert. Now Moses had to try to think up ways to convince the people to do that. And Moses would have had to face the more challenging task of how to pass this promise along to the people of succeeding generations if they were to, indeed, continue to be the people *chosen for the responsibility* to be G-d's people. Not an easy task, mister.... And Pharaoh would have dipped his oars back into the water to head for shore, already hearing in the distance some of G-d's *chosen people* muttering *tsk, tsk, tsk* to themselves as they prepared for the long trip on which G-d was about to take them—out of four hundred years of Egyptian slavery.

CHAPTER SEVEN

Finding Gold in California

It was early Friday afternoon in Los Angeles. West Coast hip; this was 1980. I'd just moved to California after working out my stand-up act in New York. I was walking on Fairfax Avenue, picking up my dry cleaning, heading back to the house in which I was living at that time on Poinsetta Drive.

Poinsetta Drive turned into Poinsettia Place, as Poinsettia Place curved onto Sunset Boulevard. And to look closely, one is Poinsetta and one is Poinsettia. And one is Drive and one is Place. I was confused enough when I first moved to California—these street names didn't help. Explaining to my friends how to get to my house was like telling my friends we would never see each other again! I'm telling you, Lewis and Clark would have given up being explorers if they would have ever been given an assignment to find these two streets.

On this particular day, I had been walking home after putting in one of my long, daily runs through the streets of Hollywood and Beverly Hills. I was wearing my usual little running outfit: tank top and running shorts. I bought some groceries, picked up my dry cleaning, grabbed the wire hanger with two fingers, slung it over my shoulder and headed to one of the above-mentioned streets. I'm sure the original city planners of Los Angeles are sitting around the nursing home now, enjoying their bowls of Cream of Wheat, still talking about the naming of these streets and laughing hysterically.

To get home, I walked up Fairfax Avenue, where the traffic was always heavy, especially on a Friday afternoon. Cars were cruising up and down the street, people were bustling up the street, down the street, across the street. It was Friday afternoon in the predominantly Jewish section of West Hollywood. There were Jewish shops, kosher pizza places, kosher falafel places, kosher bakeries, supermarkets, newsstands, everything. On Friday afternoons Jews on Fairfax prepared for Friday night Shabbat. On Friday afternoons I would walk the streets, talking to myself. Not idle talk, mind you, but going through comedy material that I'd be doing in my act that night at The Improv and The Comedy Store.

So now you know: stand-up comedians and actors talk to themselves during the day and to audiences at night. And we talk to ourselves after the shows too, to review what we talked about on stage that night and to review what we talked about to ourselves before the show! However, if you see a stand-up comedian or an actor talking to himself or herself—and they're not in any show—call the authorities.

As I passed by a Los Angeles landmark, Cantor's Delicatessen, a kosher-style restaurant on Fairfax (not kosher, but they called it kosher style, I think because every non-kosher sandwich they served came with a pickle), I noticed a table on the street set up in front of the restaurant.

A young fellow with a short black beard wearing a black hat and a black coat sitting at the table looked at me and asked me if I was Jewish. On Fairfax Avenue? Asking someone if they were Jewish? It was like asking someone at the Sioux-Dakota Tribal Pass in 1842 if they were Indian! All I could think of was why was this Amish man asking me if I was Jewish? It was the reverse of the scene in *The Frisco Kid* when Gene Wilder's character, a chassidic Jew from Eastern Europe, runs into a group of Amish men on a trail in Pennsylvania. He was so excited to see what he thought were fellow chassidic countrymen that he ran up to them yelling *"Lansmen, lansmen,"* only to realize, as he got closer, that these weren't chassidic Jews at all, but Pennsylvania Dutch Amish! Apparently from a synagogue with which he was unfamiliar!

It was the same with me. I had never had any contact with chassidim. In the vast Jewish community in which I grew up, we were told that chassidic Jews were completely separate from us and that some of them didn't even think of us as Jews. I would later learn what a myth this was. The overwhelming majority (if not all) of chassidic Jews in my experiences cherish all Jews. What the misunderstanding might be is they fervently want and hope that all Jews will become observant of Torah.

I looked at the table I was approaching, and then looked at the heavy amount of cars on the street. I was faced with a dilemma: walk past the table with this fellow with the beard and the hat or run out into the middle of the street into oncoming traffic. Hmm. I started seeing my whole life up 'til then pass in front of me, and I can tell you that some rabbis were definitely in the mix. Should I risk talking to this rabbi with the hat and the coat and the beard? Or should I free myself of the prospect of this conversation by, you know, running into traffic? As I got closer to the table, and realized that this man was definitely not from any Lancaster, Pennsylvania Amish parrish at all, I really got scared.

I continued walking toward, but not directly to, his table. I tried not to look at this fellow or at the table. I looked at the traffic. My peripheral vision picked up a bunch of religious objects on the table and I immediately started thinking about—oh, yes—what type of getting-hit-by-a-car insurance I might have!

On the table were long leather straps tied to little black boxes, and some books ... and, I think, an ice cream cup! *Oh my G-d, keep walking slowly, don't attract his attention,* I thought. In one corner of my mind it was as if I was sitting in a classroom staring straight ahead, hoping, praying the teacher wouldn't call on me. But as I tried to literally fly by the table, I got caught.

"Are you Jewish?" The fellow with the beard and the hat asked.

Oh my G-d! Is this fellow with the coat and the hat and the beard really talking to me? Or is this a flashback to my junior high school social studies teacher calling on me? Indeed, if it was my social studies teacher at Creston Jr. High School sitting there at the table, this would be the biggest turnaround to hit the New York City school system since ... ever! Headline: *Jr. High School Social Studies Teacher Goes Over the Edge—and Turns Chassidic...!* Seventh graders immediately petition the superintendent of schools to let them go from seventh grade—directly to Community College!

Well, it wasn't my junior high school teacher.... It was the fellow at the table with the beard. "Are you Jewish?" he asked again, with a smile.

It was the moment of truth. Do I lie and say no? That would have been as easy as could be. Case closed. Goodbye. No, I'm not Jewish. Bye, bye. Or do I say yes? Case opened.... I looked at him, I looked at the straps, I looked at the boxes, knowing full well what they were: *tefillin* ... and I looked at the ice cream cup. I knew the significance of the tefillin, phylacteries affixed to the arm and forehead by men (over the age of thirteen) at weekday morning prayers, but I was very curious to know what had changed in the ancient practice of Judaism that now included ritual ice cream!

While, and I do assure you, this (I imagined) newly developed practice of eating ice cream directly after putting on tefillin played only a casual (but nonetheless interesting part) in my decision of whether or not to stop at the Jews-R-Us table, the real dilemma was to decide how to answer the question of whether or not I was Jewish! And please keep in mind that darting out into oncoming Fairfax traffic was still a definite option.

I quickly realized that the next twenty seconds might not be enough time to ponder a new religious identity for myself. And I also realized that if I, indeed, decided to try a brand new religion, I would never have enough patience for the rest of my life to explain to everybody I knew—in keeping with a decision to try some new religious order that I might have seen advertised on a bus-stop bench in Encino—why I would now only wear beaded frocks and feathered turbans.

So I opted for telling the truth. I said, "Yes, I'm Jewish."

Then he asked, "Did you put on tefillin today?"

I said, "Today? What time is it? Today? I haven't put on tefillin since my bar mitzvah."

"So," he said, "let's put on tefillin right now."

"Right now?" I said, cringing to myself.

Suddenly that turban-and-frock-bus-stop-bench religion was looking pretty attractive. I was afraid to turn around since I imagined the traffic on Fairfax had stopped so that drivers could open their windows to rest their arms on the window ledge for what they knew was going to be a crucial decision in a Jew's life—and a somewhat fascinating show. People directly around me were staring at me in my little running outfit and my dry cleaning held over my shoulder wondering what I was going to do. This I was not imagining.

And while thoughts swept through my mind of the great extent of the Jewish peoples' existence, I pictured the patriarch Abraham counting the stars in the sky, representing the myriad numbers of Jews there would be someday, and I saw it all ending on Fairfax Avenue with me being asked by this young fellow with the hat and the coat and the beard—and the ice cream cup—if I'd put on tefillin that day! What could I do? I didn't want to be the one to throw Abraham's count off. So I said, "Yes, I'll put on tefillin!"

It wasn't an indecisive yes. It was a *yes, yes*! I put my dry cleaning on the table, which made for the most incongruous configuration of objects sitting next to each other on a table, ever: tefillin, religious books, a melting ice cream cup and dry cleaning from Shottenstein's French Dry Cleaners!

And before I could ask what do I do now, this young rabbi was wrapping the thin leather straps and little leather boxes all over my left arm and my forehead. And there I was, establishing the newest and presumably the most un-coolest fashion statement in all of Hollywood: running shorts, tank top, and tefillin!

With that, he led me through a prayer that I certainly remembered—the mainstay of Judaism—the *Shema*. *Shema Yisroel Hashem Elokaynu, Hashem Echod.* (*Hear O Israel: The Lord is our G-d, The Lord is One.*) It was enough to stop traffic—and make it move again!

I hadn't said the Shema since my bar mitzvah. And if you're Jewish, and you haven't said the Shema in a very long time, something can be awakened in you, something called the *Pinte L'Yid*, that inner Jewish soul spark.

ࠔ ࠒ

It was awakened in me that hot Friday afternoon on Fairfax Avenue.

I thanked him for his help as he unwrapped the tefillin from around my arm and removed it from my head. And I vividly remember slapping my wrist several times to alert my blood that, indeed, break time was now over!

Then the young rabbi told me something I had never heard before. He said that Judaism was an active religion. "We're an active people."

And he said if I was Jewish, I could be *doing Jewish*.

"Doing Jewish?" I asked.

He said, "Yes, doing Jewish."

And I thought, *Like what? Eating hamantaschen, or pronouncing the letters 'ch' like I was getting ready to get rid of some phlegm?*

And, seeming to know what I was thinking, he continued. "We've been doing things Jewish, commanded to us in Torah, all through the millennia to bring us to where we are today!"

"Let me get this straight: we've been doing Jewish things, commanded to us in Torah, that have made us wind up on ... Fairfax Avenue?"

He said, "Well, in an interesting way, yes."

"Are you sure we've been doing the right things?"

"Most definitely!"

I was scared to ask him what we'd been doing! I thought he might bring out a small biblical animal for me to sacrifice. At that moment I started mapping out in my head alternative routes home that I could take that would never bring me in contact with that table again.

"Doing what Jews do," he continued, "putting on tefillin, keeping kosher, observing the Sabbath...."

"Oh," I said. And then I thought, *Oh, no!* This young rabbi with the coat and the beard and the ice cream was making too much sense. And suddenly my memories began pushing their way forward. There was no getting around it now—I was in the La Brea Tar Pits for Jews! I knew what he was talking about and, sure, it would've been nice if I could have been doing those things he was talking about, but I wasn't willing to do so much Jewish stuff at that time. But in one part of my mind, I felt a comfort.

₭ ℂ₭

I thanked him politely, and asked him where he was from. I expected him to say from some far-off planet (with that sheet metal teacher) I'd never heard of, like Hamantaschen. He said, "Brooklyn."

This planet I'd heard of. We talked about Brooklyn (where I had gone to graduate school at Brooklyn College), I picked up my dry cleaning, and was about to go on my way when I stopped. I didn't ask him, but I was dying to know what the religious significance of the ice cream cup could be. I had never heard anything about it through the years, but I was hoping, very much, that ice cream had become a part of doing Jewish! For such a mitzvah I might have been able to make some concessions. But then, without embarrassing myself by asking him, I came to my senses. I was a bit disappointed. I was hoping I'd found an ancient Jewish sect that worshipped ice cream! *The Fairfax Cold Chassidim!* No such luck. It was just ice cream waiting to be eaten. No meaning. No lesson. Just some ice cream.

I said goodbye, and I went back to being not a practicing Jew, but a stand-up comedian, working those two shows Friday, two shows Saturday ... and those shows every other night of the week. Fairfax Avenue went back to being Fairfax Avenue before the Sabbath: Jews greeting one another, buying warm challahs and chickens galore, special Sabbath treats, and whatever else went along with Jewish people preparing for Friday night.

But I can tell you that act of putting on tefillin left me with the feeling that the part of me that I had been avoiding all through the years wasn't avoiding *me*. I didn't feel as though I was in a tar pit at all. I felt, for an instant, that I had been back home—the home where I very often did feel like I was in a tar pit. But home is home. And when I thought about that spark of Judaism inside of me, for one of the first times in my life—growing up as I did in that argumentative home—I did happen to get a good feeling that day about the fact that no matter where I might ever be in my life, I will always have a home.

And thoughts of *a candy store no more* didn't seem so crucial anymore. The Loew's Paradise and the Bronx I remembered seemed like trifles, like fool's gold, compared to the major vein in the mountain I'd been shown—where the real gold was. That's where I had to dig. Like in the movie *Treasure of the Sierra Madre* (which probably played at the Loew's Paradise) with that famous scene in it where the new prospectors thought they had found real gold when they spotted some pyrite (fool's gold). It wouldn't be that easy—they would have to go further up the mountain for the real strike.

Now I'd been shown what I should look for, what I would have to look forward to. And whether I knew it or not, I was on my way back to my Judaism. But I wasn't ready yet. I was very much in the comedy club world, working and having a great time. But with this one experience on Fairfax Avenue, I was able to see things in a different light.

CHAPTER EIGHT

Understanding By Doing

Several years passed. I continued working all over the country as a comedian, still doing television appearances, and still doing pretty much nothing Jewish. When I came back from one of my week-long bookings on the road, one cold March day in 1988 in Manhattan, I heard a familiar sound when I passed by a place called Lincoln Square Synagogue, a very well-known Modern-Orthodox Jewish Center in Manhattan. The tune I knew, but not the song. I had never heard of Lincoln Square Synagogue until then. High up on the outside wall of the synagogue was a large sign that read *Turn Friday Night into Shabbos.* I looked up at that sign, and kept looking. It seemed to be a shout-out to me. I was ready to see what it was all about. So I got a little closer. And the words *Turn Friday Night into Shabbos* (Sabbath) were like an old acquaintance that looked a little different to me. I lifted my head and thought, *Hmm, turn Friday night into Shabbos?* That sign was talking to me. Why can't I have a Shabbos? *Hmm.* And that *hmm* was the same *hmm* I knew from the Bronx. You know, every time I go *hmm* something good seems to happen. *Hmm.*

What scared me most was the word Shabbos. I remembered the word Shabbos. The word only. But now I looked at this sign as though I was a new-age camera turning those old black-and-white photos of so many Friday nights I'd known into colored pictures of Friday nights now. But it wasn't that easy, because now Friday nights were something different to me. I would spend Friday nights in night-clubs, comedy clubs. Turn Friday night into Shabbos? I wanted to get up on a ladder and change the sign to *Turn Monday Night into Shabbos!* Who works Monday nights? Night Court judges? Customer service telephone operators in India? Monday nights could be *my* Shabbos! Instead of celebrating the end of the week with a day of rest, I'll celebrate the beginning of the week with a day of rest! Yeah! I'll dress up spiffy Monday afternoons, I'll go to synagogue Monday night, I'll wonder why nobody is there; it'll be very relaxing.

So I went to the library and leafed through a book of Jewish laws, and not only couldn't I find a rationale for turning Monday night into Shabbos, I couldn't find Monday nights mentioned at all! You would think the Torah would mention Monday night somewhere! Don't slay your neighbor's ox ... on a Monday night! Try not to bring a turtle dove into the Holy Temple ... on a Monday night! But nothing! And show me in the Torah where it says that Monday night *can't* be Shabbos! What? On page number ... alright, wise guy. So Friday night it is.

℘ ℂ℟

I went to *Turn Friday Night into Shabbos*. And I loved it—the camaraderie, the genuine good feeling of belonging ... and the food! I remembered Friday nights again— but in a different way.

Judaism always seemed to be the one thing that held my family together through the verbal abuse, through the subjugation I endured, the constant strife I lived with ... Judaism seemed to be the referee.

In my family, we didn't call it Shabbos. We called it Friday night.

I remembered the food especially: the *challah* or as we called it "chally"; the kasha varnishkas; the gefilte fish; the Cel-Ray soda (celery soda—I know, it sounds vile, but it was actually quite good. It's an acquired taste, acquired by three thousand years of disruptive living. It's no egg cream, but then again egg creams don't require any sustained period of misery to taste good).

And then there was the pot roast. And the gravy in the pot roast. And the carrots and the potatoes in the gravy of the pot roast. And the prunes swishing passed the carrots and the potatoes in the gravy of the pot roast—purposefully—like special forces on a mission. And no ordinary mission, mind you. These were smart prunes, strategic prunes—pinpoint prunes. Cruise Missile prunes! They knew their target, and they waited patiently to strike. They were usually called upon at Passover time under the code name *tsimmis*. But my mother used them every week under the code name pot roast! And I remembered the chopped liver, warm—but the conversation cold.

And those were Friday nights at my home. My mother would stand at the refrigerator with a handkerchief on her head, light some candles on top of the refrigerator, wave her hands about, cover her eyes and move her lips. I never really knew what my mother was doing; she never told me, and I never asked. And that was that.

The candles, as I remembered, were in little cups, in remembrance of my grandparents. I cannot say they were Shabbos candles, but they did serve my mother well. And for that purpose it served our home well.

What I remember most definitively about Friday nights is that there was a little less yelling in the house. As a matter of fact, I think that with all the bickering and petty family squabbling, if it wasn't for Friday nights, I'm sorry to say, we might have torn each other apart emotionally.

I often used to wonder if G-d came into a house so that the conflicts would end or if the conflicts would end so that G-d could come into the house. Either way, this was the Bronx, and miraculously, G-d was there. And now years later, G-d was here. And so were Friday nights. But now, suddenly, it seemed right for me to call it not only Friday night, but Shabbos.

ℰ ℭ

At *Turn Friday Night into Shabbos* I learned about the rituals: the washing of the hands before eating bread and the blessing sanctifying the bread; the blessing sanctifying the wine; the singing, and the banging on the table in time to the singing. I'm always drumming on furniture in time to music anyhow, so why not on Shabbos? And why not to Jewish songs? I like Jewish songs. I've always liked Jewish songs.

ℰ ℭ

So with that one experience, I was on my way to becoming a rediscovered Jewish person. And whatever vocation I choose—that's just what I happen to do. That vocation can stay the same or change with the years. But my inner identity would remain. Vocations do change, and vocations are lost and other vocations are found. But who you were when you were born remains who you are. The soul you cannot change. If there are those who think you can, well, that's a question for the ages.

Every person was born somewhere. And whether we like it or not, that's where we were born. You can never, ever change that. Ever. You can wish you were born somewhere else, but you can never change where—and to whom—you were born.

Making a Decision

Aside from looking for some spiritual direction, calmness, or any thought of returning to Judaism, the underlying thought came in that if I was ever going to be able to answer questions about Judaism, by anyone, and especially young Jews, I should learn a little about it again myself. The distinct feeling that I didn't know enough about Judaism to be able to answer a young person's prospective questions bothered me terribly. I knew I could not let this stand. And it was this factor along with my work, my relationships, my disconnection to my family, my longstanding passion through the years for everything Jewish that forced me to act. Being ignorant on my own seemed fine to me. But being ignorant to a young Jew's questions about Judaism was not fine.

So after much thought and, I assure you, a lot of procrastination, I went over to a Jewish building in Manhattan that just happened to be a conservative synagogue. And I went inside. I looked on the bulletin board of the synagogue and saw a flyer: *Beginners Class in Judaism. FREE!*

My Jewish guilt reared its head again like a lion making himself known to the jungle: Learn about my Judaism again so I can renew a life-affirming connection to myself and my knowledge of the laws and rituals that has kept my people in existence for hundreds of centuries? Sure. Yeah, yeah, all that stuff's important too ... but FREE? Where do I sign up? As much as I wanted to re-connect and learn, at the outset, if this class had been three dollars for the whole semester I might've considered converting to anything-else-ism right then and there. The fact that this class was free was not really about the money. (I assure you, I've paid for many classes and lectures since then.) It was the fact that they wanted Jews to come in and learn about their Judaism without making it seem as though they were selling a class. That gave me a good feeling. I needed that. I'm sure I'm not alone in that feeling.

So I enrolled. And I loved it. With one class I could answer questions about what I learned. And I wanted to know more, so I could answer more. It enabled me to renew my interest in, my fascination with, and my passion for something that I remembered as a boy but missed out on a whole lot. It felt good. I felt connected again. It started me on the path to my way back. And did I mention it was FREE?

CHAPTER NINE

The Future Can Start Anytime

It came down to only one sure thing, that sure thing that brought me home for that brief time on Fairfax Avenue: my Judaism. Down to it—because that's where it was. Maybe I needed to find it— and bring it up to where it belonged. And in that way, it would surely bring me along with it.

℺ ℹ

A Jewish person becomes ready to explore his or her Judaism, again, when he or she is ready. And even though each Jewish person is ready at birth, what happens in between, well, just happens. Starting something new can be difficult. Turning around too quickly can be dizzying. Deciding to start is immediate; lasting change, however, is gradual.

And there is no one reason why a Jewish person decides to get closer to his or her Judaism. There are so many reasons, each one correct.

℘ ☙

For anyone: Starting a journey, starting a business, starting a new school semester, training for a marathon, running a marathon, going through medical school, climbing a mountain ... sometimes even getting up in the morning can be a drudge. Nothing's easy. And nothing should be easy. You know what's easy? Going to a restaurant and being waited on. That's easy. You know what's easy? Sitting on the couch like a zombie surfing 350 channels of television. That's easy. You know what's easy? *Twittering*! That's easy! If you're looking for easy, don't look here. Judaism is not easy. If Judaism was easy, there would be swarms of prospective converts climbing over fences to join us—if only to get off work for the Jewish holidays! No, if you think Judaism is easy, your definition of the word easy differs from the most commonly accepted definition in every dictionary on the planet. As a matter of fact, if you're not Jewish, and you're thinking of becoming Jewish—because you think it's easy—read on. There is one thing that is easy: if you're Jewish already, that's the easy part. You're there to begin with. Now it's a question of putting the key in the Rolls Royce, or letting it sit in the driveway....

℘ ☙

Value in personal spirit; value in uniquely discerning right from wrong; confidence in being connected to an ancient—and modern—people;

and value in a personal foundation—among other qualities—is Judaism. And *value* and *easy* don't mix well.

You have the right to put in your new claim on what was yours to begin with. And it doesn't matter who encourages you—it does matter that it rings true.

And encouraging yourself is as true as it gets.

℘ ℂ

You would think, if you're Jewish, with all current modes of communication available, it would be a cinch to connect up to Judaism again. And it is. Everything's there, and always has been.

But, vis-a-vis Judaism: the latest celebrities-du-jour can be around for three minutes, and attract more people to themselves, Jews included, than any synagogue or church or mosque in the world. Why? Because celebrities represent fun and fantasy and escape. And fun and fantasy and escape beat solemn every time.

Houses of worship are not usually noted for fun. You might have fun there, of a sort, but very few people are waiting for synagogues or churches or mosques to open up so they can go inside and *party down!*

Houses of worship are there for something else. And it's that something else that can carry us through life's bumps and turns.... And especially when the music stops.

℘ ℂ

Balance in a person's life is imperative. Priorities in a person's life are imperative. And each to his or her own. Do we pray to live? Or do we live to pray? I've seen people live to pray; and I've seen it work for them. I pray to live. Prayer, for me, supports my life's activities.

It centers me. It gives me balance. It gives me confidence. It gives me motivation. It inspires me. But in my sense of priorities, I would rather limit my involvement in religion and increase my life's activities than limit my life's activities to increase my involvement in religion. And even though I choose one with which to involve myself more, both my life's activities and my religion—together—give me balance. Each feeds the other. It's a lesson I've learned.

And responsibility and fun and laughter—and living very much in the secular world—is what Judaism very much supports.... Not only the traditions of Judaism, but its practice. Judaism's observance.

As described to me by chassidic rabbis I've gotten to know, Torah itself is not a history book but a guidebook.... A guidebook for, and of, the *neshama*, the Jewish soul.

And being true to Torah's daily rituals and commandments enhances the soul, and is a source of strength, a continuum of strength—wisdom that goes back more hundreds and thousands of years than our imaginations can fathom. So I always assume the Torah knows better. Respect to substance. Respect to longevity.

CHAPTER TEN

At the ...
Star-of-David Roads

After I learned about how I could turn Friday night into *Shabbos* I thought: Now what? How do I continue on this path? And why continue on this path? The why is as personal and diverse as is every Jew. And there isn't any one why. And there isn't any one way. I had my why. Now which way? Going to a class is one thing, but observance? Was I ready for that? Who knew?

If you live in the U.S. or in cities in Canada or in most other parts of the world, there are synagogues in almost every city. Some of these synagogues are parts of Jewish organizations that are very concerned with outreaching to fellow Jews. But unless you know that these organizations exist you wouldn't necessarily know they're there.

The practical truth is that synagogues are just buildings. And if there isn't a giant sign on the building like *Turn Friday Night Into Shabbos* or *Shabbat Across America*, a Jewish person walking past a building most of the year is not likely to be summoned to come inside to learn about Judaism. But if you're Jewish, and you think you've been summoned to come inside and explore your Judaism, well, then, what can I say—make sure it's a synagogue, and then—go inside! And, of course, as I did, you can choose to find a synagogue on your own. And believe me, for me, standing outside was easier than going inside. But I did.

Oh, occasionally there are men standing outside of synagogues looking for a *minyan* (a quorum of ten Jewish men needed for prayer services), but some of those men may not be thinking about you per se. They're thinking about their minyan. If you go inside, they'll thank you, show you the prayer book, wrap a *tallis* around you, strap tefillin on you (if it's in the morning, and in each case if you're a man), and leave you to pray as best you can. Sometimes one of the men will concern himself with helping you, but it's not a certainty. And they go so fast that once they get you inside and start the service, they probably won't even know you're there! No, this is not a good way to learn about your Judaism again. This is a way to probably not want to go inside a synagogue again.

℘ ℭ

But there is a way to learn about Judaism again, or for the first time. Many thousands of Jews of all ages and backgrounds, men and women, have done it, and are still doing it. A moment to look for is that moment when, as a Jew, you realize that you aren't doing anything

Jewish—but would like to. For me it was the moment I decided to find that Jewish building to go into; that synagogue offering the beginners class. And there are many synagogues like that.

It's a realization, an awareness. It might not cause someone to act at first, but it is the moment when the *spark of Judaism* wakes up. And when a person wakes up, he or she is groggy. The instinct is to go back to sleep. Try not to! Try to make it your business to look forward to Friday night—to make it a night for Jewish celebration. If you don't know where to go, again, go to a Jewish building! Not necessarily for a prayer service, but to just go inside and say hello, and simply tell them you're Jewish and that you'd like to do something Jewish, like take a class or do something Jewish on Friday night. Whether you know it or not ... you've just come back. When a fellow Jew shows a desire to find out more about classes or Friday night or the holidays—the folks at almost every synagogue, or maybe every synagogue, will be more than eager to help.

You might not fit into their particular synagogue—or you may—but they'll be more than certain to give you some good options. Not every synagogue is a comfortable fit for every Jewish person. I know I can't afford most of them! And my hair's too long for some of them. And even when I get a haircut, then my thin tie is not the right width for some of them. But it's like the old adage: seek and ye shall find ... But when you find the right synagogue that's a bit more comfortable for you ... ye shall be drinking some sweet, sweet wine and eating some fine chicken and scrumptious kugel—I can assure ye!

CHAPTER ELEVEN

Testing the Waters

While still working in the comedy clubs in New York and on the
road I somehow became the authority on Judaism in the comedy clubs
in which I worked. It seemed my mere presence would discourage comics
from using curse words (or worse) in the areas where we waited to go on
stage each night. (Moses was right; he couldn't be responsible for future
generations.) Instead of our usual conversations centering on the comedy
goings-on of the day, out of nowhere, Jewish comics would come over to
me and ask me when Yom Kippur was. And they were sincere. Or, as one
of the comics asked, "Are Boar's Head meats kosher?"

Boar's Head meats kosher? The company's logo is a picture of a
wild boar! That should be a hint right there. It's not a good marketing
idea to package kosher meats with pictures of pigs on the wrapper!

It felt good though. I was clearly in two worlds.

ഌ ര

Back in the other world, I explored different synagogues. I went uptown, downtown, across town, anywhere within walking distance on Shabbat. (And for me, as a long-distance runner, even five- or six-miles walking distance was okay.) But my main concern in going to a *shul* was not where it was but that the congregation service didn't end before I had a chance to realize it had even started! Synagogue services always go way too fast for me.

So I found myself going to shuls where I could somehow keep up with the speed of the prayers. And, of course, that severely limited the amount of shuls to which I could go. At most shuls, I couldn't keep up with the prayers at all. I read at my own pace, always in English. I did learn how to read Hebrew again, but I didn't pray in Hebrew. I could say the blessings in Hebrew after eating a meal, but not the prayers in Hebrew during the service. And I don't think it had anything to do with the speed of the prayers. I recite the after-meal blessings in Hebrew pretty fast. I think it was because I didn't want to immerse myself into the rituals too much. I wanted to keep the secular part of me intact. Praying in Hebrew seemed to carry me too much over to the other side. I very much wanted to be a part of it, but I didn't want it to envelop me. And that's the way I am to this day: wholly secular, but also observant. But I can tell you, praying in Hebrew during services, if I only could, would be much more elevating and much more spiritually fulfilling. It's preferable. Maybe someday.

At the shuls where I could keep up with the prayers, like at Lincoln Square Synagogue, I was okay. They had (and still have) a Beginners Minyan service, led by the very dedicated and personable Rabbi Ephraim Buchwald. I went there week after week on Saturday mornings because of the learning and the camaraderie. I know I probably shouldn't say it, but part of the reason I went there also, I think, was because it started later than the regular service! That 3,300 years—and a half-hour—made quite a difference! That's a hint to all synagogues: to attract fellow Jews, start later!

At the shuls where the congregation recited the prayers like cars doing laps at the Indy 500, I was not okay. But I did my best. They would finish five or ten minutes before me, but I would always say all the words in the prayers and finish at my own pace. And still do.

After solving the dilemma of the ping-pong match prayer races, I was confronted with another shul challenge: lifting the *Sefer Torah* (the parchment Torah scroll read at a service with a minyan).

I dreaded, and still do, the *gabai* ([pronounced gab-eye] the one who helped with all the detailed work of keeping the service moving fast), looking around for the next congregant, who would be called up to the Torah to bless and to read (or have it read by the one who reads from the Torah scroll) the next chapter or section of the *parsha* (portion of the Torah).

I would sit there looking down like an ostrich with its head in the sand, hopefully conveying the message, "Please don't call on me, please don't call on me!"

Then, out of the corner of my eye, I would see a pair of shoes heading my way, and think: "Please, shoes, keep walking!"

"What's your Hebrew name?" the gabai attached to the shoes would ask.

I was looking down, pretending to be asleep. How did this guy find me? "Reuven," I would say.

"And your father's Hebrew name?" he would ask.

What, is this guy writing a book? "Nasan," I would say, which was my father's name.

Then he would call me up to the *bima* (the stand where the Sefer Torah was read during services), I would say the blessing, then the one who was reading from the Sefer Torah would read, and after he would finish, they would congratulate me! *What did I do?* I'd think.

"*Yishar koach*," everyone who shook my hand would say (roughly translated: good job).

Yes, I am a rather good watcher of someone who is reading aloud from an intricate, ancient parchment scroll in Hebrew! I can watch with the best of them! Of course, everybody else would be watching too; but they were watching to make sure he didn't make any mistakes in wording or pronunciation. And they would correct him if he did. But somehow these other—quality watchers—just couldn't do it without me! And when the reader was finished he said, "Yishar koach" to *me*! It was then that I re-thought the rough translation of yishar koach to mean: *Thank you very much for not getting in the way!*

After I would be called up to the bima for what's known as an *aliah*, and my crucial participation complete, I would sit back down with the rest of the congregation—relieved that I had served my time. I wouldn't have to go back up to the bima anymore. One aliah per congregant, per reading.

Of course, it's considered an honor to be called up to the Torah for an aliah. But with everyone looking at me and yishar koaching me—for not knowing what I was doing—the esteemed honor of staying seated in that ostrich position would have been just fine!

When all the readings were finished, on different occasions, what I really dreaded was an aliah to lift up the Sefer Torah from the bima before it was returned to the ark. Unlike the other aliahs—with this aliah you could get physically hurt! Yes, I was actually frightened. I would hold my head down, look into the prayer book deep in thought and think, I'm not here, please don't call on me, go away, just because my mother was Jewish and her mother was Jewish and all their mothers before them were Jewish doesn't necessarily mean that I'm....

"What's your Hebrew name?" the executioner/gabai would ask!

"My Hebrew name? Ralph."

"What's your Hebrew name," he would politely ask again. (These were very polite executioners, with senses of humor like ... executioners!)

Inside I was answering, *You got me, you insect!* I finally answered, "Reuven ... ben Nasan."

"Would you like to lift up the Sefer Torah?" he would ask.

Inside I'd be thinking: *Are you out of your execution mind? There isn't anything in the world I'd rather do less!*

Outside I'm saying: "Sure."

And I would begin the long, slow walk to the *bima* chopping block; accompanied, in my mind of course, by extremely mellow, lethargic organ music. I'd stand in front of the Sefer Torah, which was lying flat on the bima (the music in my mind would stop), I'd grab the two wooden handles, roll out the scroll on either side, lift it up—and imagine I'd soon be headed backwards into the crowd that was patiently waiting to wish me a massive yasher koach! And with that, I'd be thinking: *Medic, medic! Is anyone in the crowd hurt? I am so sorry! I lost my balance. It was too heavy! There are so many words in there!*

But it never happens. I lift up the Sefer torah and swirl it around slowly so that everyone can see it, and then I put it back on the bima.

I did it! *I didn't fall down! No one was hurt by a flying Sefer Torah! The sacred scroll didn't rip in half! I did it! Nobody wound up wearing a Sefer Torah!* And then came the shower of yishar koachs! At least this time it was deserved! I actually had to do something for this shower. My lifting and showing skills proved to be exemplary. I survived the only aliah in a shul that risked the possibility of somebody going to the emergency room! Little did they know that by calling me up to the bima—to do anything—everyone was at risk.

And now the really scary part. I had to sit in the chair holding the Sefer Torah while the rabbi said a few words. And even sitting down, holding it, these Sefer Torahs are heavy! Also, saying that a rabbi is going to say only a few words is like saying Niagara Falls gushes moisture!

CHAPTER TWELVE

The Cholent Affair

The most bizarre of all possible bizarre shul experiences culminated, for me, one scorching July *Shabbos* at a local synagogue for my first-ever synagogue Shabbos lunch. Outside it was 105 degrees, inside it was about 112 degrees, and my temperature was a refreshing 98.6 degrees. I wasn't sweating yet, but most of my internal organs were beginning to conspire with each other to leave the body if some coolant wasn't introduced quickly!

As the meal after the services started, we sanctified the wine (kiddush) by saying the proper blessing; we ritually washed our hands before the meal; we sat down at the tables; we sanctified the bread with the blessing ... and we started eating. This eating movement prompted the sweating. I began wondering, along with the blessings over the wine and the bread, if there was a proper blessing for sweat.

The room temperature soared with the slightest movements. Cold wine, cold salads, cold fish all teetered on the brink of spoiling before they even reached the table. Plastic forks were melting. People were fanning their forks in a frantic cooling motion so that the forks would keep their shape in order for everyone to be able to pick up a piece of on-the-verge-of-going-rancid food. Before each person had a chance to put his or her fork into a piece of fish, the prongs of the forks were sticking out every which way—north, south, east and west. A fork was put into a piece of lettuce, and a cucumber would show up. It wasn't up to us what we would eat. The melted curled-up forks decided what we would eat. People were afraid to put these fishing-tackle-like forks in their mouths for fear of winding up as the catch of the day.

And the handles would be, how can I describe it—sizzling to the touch! Sizzling! I know I may have been rather subtle here, but have I made my point? *It was hot in that room!* We didn't know where the heat of the day started and the cold appetizers left off.

And then we sang songs—in Hebrew. Songs with words, I imagined, of how hot it was in that room. With every Hebrew lyric, I didn't need anyone to tell me what the song was about. I translated each lyric for myself: *Oy, it's hot! Boy, it's hot! Ayayayaya, get me, please, a damp cloth!* Then, we clapped our hands in time to the music—we would purposely miss—so we could get the full effect of the breeze from the unfulfilled claps! I couldn't believe it. No air conditioner, no fan. People were delirious! One person got up and spoke a few words from the Torah on the theme of how much time the Israelites had spent in the desert. I thought, *Aren't there any passages in the Torah of how the Israelites once went skiing in Vermont?*

Everyone was reaching for the pitchers of water and seltzer bottles on the table. I was hoping the fire department would converge on the place to give us each a hose down! But apparently the fire department has this silly rule that there actually has to be a fire for them to show up and squirt water ... not just heat!

ℰℭ ℭℛ

What did show up was a giant silver bowl, plopped onto the table by someone from the kitchen. (I suspect there was no air-conditioning in the kitchen either.) He looked like he had just smeared vaseline all over his face. The bowl was filled with some kind of ... food. And it was bellowing huge amounts of steam. Not unusual since everything in the room was bellowing huge amounts of steam! But this steam was different. There was definitely steam coming out of this molten food on purpose, like opening the door of a sauna bath in the middle of an ice rink. Big steam! And backdraft too. Everyone gasped "Wo," in unison. Wo, I guessed, must have been the Chinese word for steam! But in this context, I guessed it was also the *Hebrew* word for steam (it's not.) I had never seen anything like it. I looked inside the giant bowl. It looked like a Bessemer Converter filled with beans, potatoes, onions, meat, and, I didn't see it, but I had a feeling there was some iron ore in there too. I mean it looked like everything that was a thing was in that steaming bowl. I looked forward to a good amount of finished steel to be readied by that process at any moment.

The only thing I could assume was that everything on *Shabbat* was for a purpose. But I couldn't imagine what the purpose of delivering a steaming cauldron—of supposedly edible things—to a lunch table on a blistery hot July summer's day in New York could be all about. It looked like something they would serve in the middle of winter in eighteenth-century Romania.

୧୦ ୯୧

That's exactly what it was. It was something called *cholent*: a mix of everything except, well, iron ore! It was a combination of everything I mentioned above, plus anything else that was considered nourishing and tasty that accompanied meat in a mixture that could stretch a long way. The idea was that there should be enough cholent for everybody at the tables and for anybody who might drop by. It was a meal that started cooking on the stove before Shabbos started, without being stirred on Shabbos, and ladled out about twenty hours later at lunch. Cholent! It was nourishing, it was good, and in eighteenth-century Romania or Russia or Hungary or Poland, where many large families struggled to put food on the table, it went a long way and it was affordable. Even today, it's affordable and it goes a long way. I found out the hot way— in July! —that all through the year there should be something hot to eat Shabbos day, when initiating cooking is not to be done.

And I saw, and I learned that afternoon, that even on a swelteringly hot day in July, in a swelteringly hot room, I could be with fellow Jews, sing songs and eat bubbling hot cholent—and get a warm feeling inside that more than made up for the heat.

CHAPTER THIRTEEN

Moving in Both Worlds

It was 1989, eight years since my time in California. I thought back and remembered that young rabbi outside Cantor's Delicatessen. He would have been proud. I was on the path of *doing Jewish*. And sweating for it as well!

I started going to Friday night *Shabbat* dinners—but I also kept working in the comedy clubs on Friday nights (and all the other nights). As I started learning more and more about Shabbos observance, I stopped working on *some* Friday nights so I could enjoy more of Shabbos. I also started eating more and more on Friday nights. I mean, a lot more: chicken, potato *kugel*, challah, cake, chopped liver—anything that looked like it might be food would receive a visit from me! (But I'm a long-distance runner with three New York City marathons under my belt, so don't worry; on me, the *kreplach* is hard to spot.)

And as I kept enjoying my re-connection to my Judaism, I toyed with the idea of keeping kosher again. What was wrong with keeping kosher? I always thought it was quite beautiful.

So I asked my new friends to help. They said it was simple. When I went to the supermarket I was to look for products with an *OU* on the package. (I didn't know they meant an O with a U in the middle (the acronym for Orthodox Union, a kosher certification organization). For two months I ate nothing but soup! There's an *OU* in it! I bought Shout detergent! When my friends saw me they said it looked like I was losing a lot of weight, but they said my clothing seemed unusually clean! I said, "Yes, because all I'm doing is eating soup and washing clothes!"

Then they told me that *OU* is probably a little too advanced for me and that I should simply look for products with a *K* on the package. For two months I ate *Kix Cereal*. There's a big *K* on the box! What did I know? On Shabbos I'd have *Special K!* I figured a special day called for a special cereal!

Well, I finally figured the whole thing out, and as I started learning more about Jewish observance in general, I pretty much found myself practicing it quite naturally. One by one I replaced non-kosher foods with kosher foods. Quite easy nowadays. And I also added material to my stand-up act, as I began performing for Jewish outreach organizations that reflected the path I was on. The *OU* bit is one of them. The new Jewish outreach show I developed, *Comedy and Coming Home,* took me out of the 1990s and into 2000 and beyond, all over the United States—and to Canada, England, Belgium, and Australia, for such organizations as Chabad, Young Israel, Chicago Torah Network and The Association for Jewish Outreach Programs.

And it continues.

എ 03

I prepared for Shabbos on Fridays. I looked forward to it. And I felt good. Prayer became easier because it was meaningful and interesting. I was motivated. I actually enjoyed it. And still do.

Then somebody suggested that I try a synagogue in my neighborhood led by a very special young rabbi and his family. I went there, met the rabbi, and somehow immediately felt at home. The young rabbi had a full beard, and wore a black coat and a black hat. I thought: *Where have I seen that before?*

As we talked more and more, he answered my questions one by one. It seemed as if a friend had appeared to help me through this time in my life when I was trying to make sense of my work as a comedian, and of myself.

I kept going back to the synagogue in my neighborhood—a Chabad-Lubavitch shul—and the rabbi soon became my good friend.

We talked more and more through the months, and after many Shabbat dinners at his home, and at the shul, with his growing family and with other fellow Jews, I told him about my time in California, and about the young fellow who helped me put on tefillin on Fairfax Avenue that Friday afternoon. He asked me when that was. I told him. He told me that he had been assigned to a table, in rotation along with a couple of other students outside Cantor's Delicatessen, during that same time period. I asked him if he was from Brooklyn. He said he was. And I just looked at him, not saying a word, reliving the picture in my mind of putting on tefillin that day.

Whereas there's no way of knowing for sure if he was the same fellow that Friday afternoon—with all the information unfolding as it did—we both were as certain as could be that he was the rabbi with the hat and the coat and the beard (and I'm positive that cup of ice cream too!) who helped me with the tefillin that day. It was him! I was there and he was there! It was him! I had somehow come home again.

His name is Rabbi Shlomo Kugel.. (Yes, spelled the same way as the potato soufflé!) And as certain as we can be, the same rabbi who gave me the idea that I could *do Jewish* was now, years later, by an interesting coincidence (and not only an interesting coincidence but possibly an incredibly astounding coincidence!), a friend and a mentor.

As much as I hear about G-d's hand being present in our lives, and that there's a divine plan, and that there are no coincidences, every time I think of it—and I know this is not what the rabbis would like to hear as a testimonial to faith and observance—but every time I think of it, I get the heebie-jeebies! Even though I don't take every coincidence as a life-changing event, it did change the way I look at coincidences forever.

In my time of transition, I thought about one of the well-known bands I had been the opening act for at arenas like *Westbury Music Fair* (that first time especially, with the big man following me down the corridor to the stage) and for many, many other venues, the *Little River Band.* They proved to have a great influence on me—and on my Judaism too. I didn't know them to be Jewish, which I don't think they are—they're from Australia! At that time I didn't think there were any Jews in Australia because I always thought it was just too far away! But watching the *Little River Band* at those famous arena venues we'd be performing at, I used to sit in the back of each theater and after I had performed my portion of the show I would listen to them sing their hit song each night, "Cool Change," with the words *I know that it's time for a coo-oo-ool change.* Those words stayed with me, then, and through the stage in my life I was going through now. Maybe it was just a coincidence. I can't help thinking that maybe these coincidences just won't leave me alone! I began to think, maybe ... thank G-d.

CHAPTER FOURTEEN

From Fast Lane to Changing Lanes

I was transformed. I was able to continue to do what I was doing, working all of the nights of the week except Friday nights, and I realized I was also onto something which was guiding me towards who I really was. When I was asked questions about Judaism by young people and my peers more and more, I knew the answers more and more.

In continuing my work doing shows in New York, on television and on the road, I made a couple of appearances on a television show called *Caroline's Comedy Hour.* For the first show that was booked, I was to do a seven-minute stand-up comedy monologue.

They called me to talk about the show, and gave me the time of 3 p.m.—that Saturday—for my technical rehearsal. The show was to be taped that night. I asked them to please change my tech rehearsal time because I couldn't make it in the afternoon. (The Sabbath ended at that time of year at about 6 p.m.) They couldn't believe what I was asking! They said the tech rehearsal time was what it was, and if I couldn't make it at that time I couldn't be on the show. So I told them that I wouldn't be able to do the show, and told them why. They couldn't believe that either.

"You'd give up being on the show because of the Sabbath?" they asked.

And, albeit reluctantly, I said, "Yes."

Now they really couldn't believe it! They said they'd get back to me, and hung up the phone. I thought I'd lost the chance to be on the show for sure. But about fifteen minutes later they called me again and said that it would be all right for me to come in between 6:30 p.m. and 7 p.m. for my portion of the tech rehearsal. I thanked them, and felt as proud of myself as could be for not wavering. I didn't know I had it in me. But I did. It was the first test of my commitment to the Sabbath, and, whether reluctantly or not, I passed the test. I enjoyed the Sabbath, I enjoyed doing the show that Saturday night, and I felt great.

ස ⬀

I felt a growing confidence in myself that surprised me. I had never been a very confident person at all. But I guess I was. We learn new things about ourselves every day.

In keeping with that thought, I met an old friend of mine who's Jewish, but not observant, and never knew me as being someone interested in observant Judaism. We talked about old times and then—as it always seemed to come up in every conversation with Jewish friends then—he asked me about my observance. I don't like to go into much detail, unless, of course, someone specifically asks me to, but he asked me something that made me think a bit. He asked me the clichéd question: Is Judaism a crutch? I had been wondering that myself. I thought a bit, and then I said something that sounded quite right to me: "Judaism isn't a crutch; Judaism is a foundation." It was like one of those rainbow/halo moments, with harp music and a glow. It sounded great. And, I assure you, it impressed me more than him. But I can't help thinking that it made some impression on him as well. And as we parted, I hoped he would pass it along to his daughter.

The transformation I went through—and continue to go through—is something called *teshuva*. When I first heard this term *teshuva*, I thought they were saying *do over*. In many ways that's exactly what it is. In many religions it's termed Repentance. In Judaism it's termed Return.... And, more specifically, returning to oneself. And if you were born Jewish, well, that's who you'd be returning to! *Yourself*.

Again, it's not easy. Nothing of value is. It takes work and it takes discipline and it takes determination. It takes wanting to reclaim your place with a people. *Your* people.

I've seen advertisements here and there for tracing peoples' lineage that say, "You don't have to know what you're looking for, all you have to do is start looking."

Well, with Judaism, it's more specific: you do know what you're looking for. It's just that most people don't know how to start looking.

80 CS

People might decide to explore their own religions, when they're ready to, for any number of reasons; for Jews, guilt is not low on the list!

Finding a way back to, in our case, Judaism, is like finding something hidden, tucked away, sitting somewhere in an attic or a drawer. You couldn't find it because—you weren't looking.

I didn't happen to find my way back to my Judaism because of guilt; although, that seems to be a most prevalent way to do it. Just walk into any synagogue and start *kvetching*, blaming yourself for the economy, global warming, the Balkans War, anything! You'll undoubtedly get a sincere hug from someone and the warm greeting, "Welcome, *reb Yid!*" And you're in!

I didn't know a thing about the laws of Judaism, the rituals or the real meaning of the Holidays. I knew the most commonly held general practices of the Jewish holidays that any non-practicing, non-observant Jew growing up Jewish would know. Are you beginning to see a trend here? The vast extent of my ignorance and casual understanding of a 3,300-year-old religion? I was what Judaism's ancient sages would have termed an imbecile! Of course, in keeping with our sages' years-old practice of engaging in thought, research, and debate before reaching a definite conclusion, I'm sure they would have still come up with the same conclusion in this matter: imbecile! (But in Hebrew, I'm glad to say, it does sound more astute.)

In my early years, I got through the High Holy Days by placing my own logic on them. I believed fasting for one day on Yom Kippur was an appropriate punishment for sinning all year. I could live with that. One day? I could do that standing on my head. And since I usually only fasted for about two hours anyhow, sinning all year—and not eating for a couple of hours—to me, would be my projected way of life for many years to come! Halleluiah!

Now back down to earth, I've learned that fasting on Yom Kippur has nothing to do with punishment at all. As a matter of fact, Yom

Kippur has nothing to do with punishment. It has to do with a chance at freeing yourself from being held back by transgressions you might have been doing all year. But what do us sinners know?

I found myself defining Judaism by its limitations: fasting, praying, do this, don't do that. The whole thing was not a religion to me; it was a sentence! Why anyone would want to come back to this incarceration was beyond me.

But I knew there had to be more to the whole affair than fasting on Yom Kippur. *Turn Friday Night Into Shabbos* was the enabler, the taste (literally); the continuation of wrapping on tefillin on Fairfax Avenue that Friday afternoon. The sights and sounds and experiences on the journey back are, well, the journey. The continuing journey. The Jewish peoples' journey....

CHAPTER FIFTEEN

Shabbos Island

Imagine a race with no finish line. Good luck. Let us know when you get there. Stop signs. Traffic lights. A horse's reigns. The end of a movie. The days of the week. Nothing can go on forever. Sometimes the days of the week seem to. Everybody finds some time, mostly on the weekends, to relax a little, to slow down, and step back from the weekday drudge. But is that enough? Does that work? Stepping back a little? Sometimes it's like cleaning up a room full of spilled paint with a napkin. Clearly, something more is worth looking at.

In all our lives, we can probably safely say that the workweek, much of the time, seems to go on like spilled paint. One uphill challenge after another: like a workweek in which a school teacher is trying to teach a class of students that have their minds set on text messaging rather than what the teacher is trying to teach. Or a workweek in which longtime employees of a company are told that upcoming layoffs will be inevitable.

Also, it seems like every week that work, family, personal and financial problems are on our minds twenty-four seven. And it goes on and on, every day, every week—for pretty much everyone. An endless array of tasks and problems.

There simply has to be a respite from all this mish-mosh; a respite, preferably, with nuclear-rest capability.

A two-week vacation might seem the perfect remedy. For two weeks, that is. But when the two weeks are up ... then what? Nothing nuclear about a two-week vacation; unless it's in Vegas—or Chernobyl. But that can't really help with the workweek when we get back because—remember?—what happens in Vegas, stays in Vegas. Two weeks in Vegas, or anywhere, is just putting off the inevitable return to the problems of the workweek when you get back. It's temporary fun. And don't think one night in Bangkok will be any different. Well, it will be different, but when it's all over it's back to the same-old, same-old—more weekdays ahead.

How about a Sunday picnic. Perfect! Pack a lunch, sit by the lake, eat some lovely picnic food and think about ... *work*! No, that's not going to work. WORK! This workweek *chaos-athon* seems never-ending! What to do? Where to go? Nowhere. Stay put! Don't go anywhere. Maybe once, don't go frantically searching for a respite—let a respite come to you. (Oh, so sneaky. But stay with it....)

The Real Case for the Sabbath

Unlike Las Vegas, what happens on the Sabbath will not stay only with the Sabbath, but it will stay with you all week. There is a scene in the classic western *Shane* about a gunfighter who fights on the side of good. On a Saturday night, the range folk get together for a social dance. Faced with tough, violent adversaries every day trying to move them off their homesteads, they relax by dancing to some simple down-home music while, yes, enjoying a glass of punch! Sounds corny, huh? Well, it is. And their lives were more real and more complicated than most of our lives will ever be. Corny, once in a while, can be quite relaxing and quite cool.

Granted, religion is not one of the things that is thought of as cool. But one of the problems with religion's image is that religion's got the worst publicist on the planet: turmoil! Part of the image of religion is the image of strictness and fanaticism and hatred and violence. And, as we know, it's not always just an image. But it always seems to be in the image forefront.

The reality of religion, for the most part, though, is simply good people determined to live *just* lives. But the suspicions of each other's religions does make for mistrust and anger. There is one referee, one time-out that's called. A stop-the-clock whistle. Without question, all religions respect the Sabbath. But one of the problems is that most religions mostly respect their own Sabbath.

The Sabbath is Worth a Try

The Sabbath is not a weekday, and it's not a weekend either. In Judaism, it's not a Saturday. It's the Sabbath. And being a part of it means living in it and observing its parameters. It's that social contract between the individual, G-d, and community. And keeping the Sabbath affects each of these entities.

శౚ ౭

When I first started learning about Jewish observance, every restriction was an annoyance. If I was to observe the laws of the Sabbath, I couldn't work on Friday nights; I couldn't watch television; I couldn't take a bus or a subway or ride in a car; I couldn't cook anything; I couldn't even boil water! (That was okay because it was never one of my strong suits anyhow.) I couldn't go into a store to buy anything; I couldn't answer the phone or make a call or use the computer; I couldn't even open my e-mails! How the Jews of the exodus in ancient Egypt were expected to leave Egypt without first opening their emails is unfathomable! *Oh, that's right*, I thought again. *Email wasn't invented until after the exodus.* Amazing. Jews have been around, yes, even longer than e-mails. Come to think of it, we Jews have been around longer than mail! Something must be working. And maybe what's working is that one day a week of not working.

శౚ ౭

Being restricted in one area can make for freedom in another. Maybe, in my life, restrictions were necessary to be able to explore other areas of my life that would do me some good. I think by moving too fast in my life, what I needed most were some stop signs.

On the Sabbath, not answering the phone, making a phone call, e-mailing, or texting after a while wasn't a restriction. It was a freedom! I would look forward to the one day in the week when I would not have to immerse myself in these, sometimes— well, much of the time— trivial pursuits.... Even with my usual constant barrage of phone calls, e-mails, and texts throughout the week, I never missed a call or an email or a text. Once people became aware that I observed the Jewish Sabbath, it affected their calling and their e-mailing and their texting more than mine. Of course, life emergencies always take precedence over the Sabbath and Jewish holidays. But it was then and there that I was very comforted to realize that the barrage of calls, texts, and e-mails seemed to rarely be emergencies. These communications seemed to always be able to wait until after the Sabbath or Jewish holiday. Real freedom at last to postpone the barrages—and to enjoy the Sabbath, or the holiday.

I would work extra hard during the week—especially on Thursdays and Fridays—to finish what I needed to finish before sundown on Friday, when I knew I couldn't do any more work for that week. When I wasn't sticking to this structure, I would let things go until the following week—and I would usually let things go until the week after that also. It was like not opening mail for one day, then the next day there would be two days' mail ... and so on. After a while the mail just piles up—as do other things. Weeks don't become weeks anymore, but just amorphous time. Postmarks on letters reflect days that passed weeks ago. There was no real separation from the week—and so, I never experienced renewal. But when I knew I had to finish everything before sundown on Fridays, I did. We always work harder when we have a deadline.

$$\mathcal{SO} \ \mathcal{CR}$$

The Sabbath forbids all work, and work is not even to be talked about. We get home from work, or stop work, on Friday, and that's it. The workweek is over! Start preparing for the Sabbath! Again ... the workweek is over! Something new is about to begin. And it's not a simple Friday night off. It's a higher zone. A zone right after twilight. Literally. It's a time when the television hasn't been invented yet. Electric lights can be set to go on and shut off automatically. There are no harsh words spoken. And if we choose to adhere to these ways of the Sabbath we also take the good side effects that come along with it. All other parts of our lives become touched by it as well. It's said that, *As goes the Sabbath, so goes the week.* And what happens on the Sabbath ... does stay on with the coming week.

If we can discipline ourselves to obey the requirements of the Sabbath, it's more likely that discipline will become a part of our lives in general. We learn to discipline ourselves during the separation, for the purpose of elevating ourselves to a higher state of renewal. The more pronounced the separation, the more gratifying the renewal.

Using the lessons of the Sabbath—which enrich the Sabbath—can take us to a new level of richness back in our workweek.

There is a saying: *Absence makes the heart grow fonder.* Love is built, not only by the time we spend *with* someone but also by the time we spend *away* from someone. It's all separation and renewal. A love lesson from the Sabbath. (But be careful, too much absence can also make the heart go, "Where is he [or she] already...?" Don't stay away too long!)

&) CR

Limitations and restrictions can be constructive. Sometimes we can actually build something faster by building it slower. And sometimes we can build it better by, every now and then, simply setting it aside.

You would think that working seven days a week would bring in more money than working five or six days a week. And it just might. Money can buy things. And money can allow for a more secure life. All these points are reasonable. And another point that's reasonable is that money can buy happiness—temporary happiness.

The workweek puts money in the bank—the Sabbath puts something else in the bank. Money is to spend, spirituality is to keep. Observing the Sabbath might limit income in the short run, but with a new sense of purpose and focus and sense of self—and the self-confidence in meeting the challenge of Will that the Sabbath inherently instills—it will provide a means to tap into resources to increase income in the long run. I learned that the workweek gives us what we *think* we need, and the Sabbath defines and makes clear what we *really* need. I've never heard of anyone looking forward to a miserably encumbering workweek, but I always hear people looking forward to a fun, soulful, spiritually elevating Sabbath.

১৩ ৫৩

With my observance came a new realization for myself that everything breaks down into the physical and the spiritual, the temporary and the permanent. For everything physical, there is a spiritual counterpart. Look for it.

A beautiful thought I've experienced, through my teachers of *chassidus*, is that with Jewish observance our purpose on earth is to infuse everything physical with the spiritual. Wouldn't that be nice. Imagine using everything physical for a G-dly purpose. That's a pretty high level of thinking and of service. In my associations with chassidim of various movements, particularly Chabad-Lubavitch, and countless very spiritual non-chassidic and non-observant Jews, as well, it's a pretty interesting and admirable goal—a goal to keep looking toward.

We should always feel encouraged. When I think at times that everything might be lost, I think about the fact that a ship that's foundering is permanent—but a ship that's changing course is only temporary. Just find the right course, and make that permanent.

Lessons I learned.

ဆ ☞

And so now, every weekend, I happen to go back to a people. My people. I go to a place where there's order and sense and calmness and singing and rhythm and laughter and joy and hope and spiritual nourishment. And food and wine and "chally."

It's a place where unfounded hatreds and pettiness are set aside.

And whatever happens during the workweek, I always know that I'm going away that weekend.

Travel nice and slow.

Find the gifts some people left for me

A long time ago.

It's exotic and it's quiet

You can hear yourself go, *ahh.*

It's a place called Shabbos Island

At a spot called *neshama* (the Jewish soul).

CHAPTER SIXTEEN

Right Time, Wrong Place

One of the first and most difficult challenges I had in confronting, well, myself, was dealing with my relationships. Mainly my relationships with women. Jewish men confronting their relationships with women? There are probably no books about it because Jewish men don't want to confront their relationships with women! It wasn't a deciding factor, but it was one factor pushing me closer to my Judaism.

What was the fascination with non-Jewish women? Fair question. To Jewish men, *shiksas* (non-Jewish women) are like voodoo dolls. If we somehow want to subconsciously hurt our Jewish mothers, we don't have to stick pins in a likeness of our mothers—all we have to do is hold hands with a shiksa. Our mothers will automatically stand a good chance of developing arthritis—in the same hand we're using to hold hands with the shiksa. If there was such a thing as *Kosher Voodoo*, this would be it. Why no stick-pins in "Kosher Voodoo"? Because in keeping with Jewish Dietary Laws, "Kosher Voodoo" would have to be done in the most humane way possible.

Now please don't get me wrong, we love our devoted Jewish mothers. But at the base of this devotion is a wide range of troubled—okay, doomed—Jewish mother-son relationships. At the very core of this hodgepodge upbringing is every Jewish mother's smoldering, inner-right-of-passage-self-proclaimed-entitlement: *I gave birth to you therefore I can use you like a dump truck on a chain gang!*

But even entangled in this fray, Jewish men don't really want to consciously hurt our Jewish mothers. We probably don't even want to *subconsciously* hurt them. It's a deeper level than that. It's a sub-subconscious level. Call it payback—or call it payback—or call it ... it's payback, there's no two ways about it! It's subterranean, sub-subconscious payback!

We use this convenient device of payback because we also subconsciously very much want to find out what all this clamor is about going out with a shiksa! Blonde hair, cute as a peach, not neurotic! What's that all about? Not neurotic? How is it possible that a human being cannot be neurotic? Well, we want to find out about that. And when we see that going out with a shiksa doesn't actually kill our Jewish mothers, it does give us some peace. Developing arthritis—as opposed to death—is a very compassionate trade-off that Jewish men are very happy to do for the women in our lives who, we've convinced ourselves, are mostly responsible for making us the way we are! Forget the fact that there might be a million and one other factors for us being the way we are—as soon as Jewish boys hit the later teen years they're already plotting to show up at home holding hands with a six-foot-tall Baptist girl named Mary Grace, who would head straight for the kitchen to cook up a possum-crawfish dinner in a *milchik* (dairy) pot while encouraging the family to join her in a rousing chorus of *Bringing in the Sheaves!* We don't care what all the other factors are! This display should do the trick nicely. Well now, with all these goings-on, it seems that Mom's joints do appear to be acting up; Mary Grace, would you be a dear, and get the Aleve?

The Jewish Family Game: Blame the Victim!

Well, now that the shiksa parade has been explained here—not totally eliminated here yet, but at least explained—there still remain some real Jewish family questions that are worth exploring. They're all in the mix of making a Jewish person a Jewish person.

Many Jewish (and I'm sure other) parents blame their own hardships and shortcomings on their children, because it seems the children are simply there. I mean, it's more convenient to lash out at their own family member than to knock on a neighbor's door and start yelling at *their* children! Besides, there are severe consequences following that route; immediate consequences. Blaming your own children has delayed consequences.

A shame of many Jewish parents, and, I'm sure, parents in general, is taking children for granted. We assume that children don't see what's happening, and that children don't know. I've got news for you, and I'm not the only one who's got this news for you. The next time you flagrantly berate a child or casually order them about or take their feelings for granted, please know that they see, and they know. Just because a child can't tell you what's on his or her mind, doesn't mean they don't see or don't know.

It's not guaranteed that a child will react to respect with respect, but it is guaranteed that children will react to disrespect with disrespect. It doesn't always show up in words. It doesn't always show up at all. But it's always there. And the respect—or disrespect—might last a lifetime.

So stay close to your children every day. Nurture the relationship. Respect it.... And respect them. You'll be honored.

Oh Yes, Back to the Matter at Hand

I strayed from Jewish women. I was told not to—so I did. It was not a discussion with my parents; it was a rule. As a matter of fact, there was little discussion with my parents on any matter.

A girlfriend of mine was an adorable, talented, sensible Methodist girl from a fine Methodist family with roots in East Texas. You think it's hard to translate Yiddish into English? Try translating a fine Methodist family with roots in East Texas into Yiddish! It can't be done. Instead, I tried to translate the relationship into something workable. A Jewish man and a Methodist woman. It can be done. Or so I thought. But something gets lost in the translation. And what was lost was, ultimately, how to make it work—while staying true to who each of us were.

Any compatible relationship between a man and a woman of different religions can work—if the couple is on a bit of a vacation mode from discussing shared backgrounds and beliefs. But as soon as everything is brought into reality mode, that's when something gets lost in the translation. It's like traveling toward a fork in the road: one road Judaism, the other not. One partner, or both, has to give in, and give up *something* in order to continue traveling together. It's done all the time. But from a Jewish point of view, it's almost always at the expense of Judaism.

ℬ ℭ

This particular relationship went well throughout the year until a Jewish holiday would come around. It was easier when a Christian holiday would come around; there's relatively nothing to do. Easter? Buy her a bonnet, paint some eggs. Christmas? Buy her a present, sing some Christmas songs—written by Irving Berlin, a Jew!—and it's still holiday magic time. But the Jewish holidays? Watch out! There are no eggs to paint, no bonnets to buy, no songs to sing, except cantorial music and, of course, the song *Exodus*, written by Pat Boone, a non-Jew! (I don't know who wrote the song "Dreidel, Dreidel, Dreidel, I Made it Out of Clay," but I'm going to be seriously looking into my maternal ancestry if I find out that "Dreidel, Dreidel, Dreidel" was written by Pat Boone!) No, there was nothing to be shared when the Jewish holidays came around except ritual and guilt!

When the Jewish holidays were with us I always felt as though I should be doing something that I wasn't doing. Passover? Shouldn't I be at a Seder? Shouldn't I be eating matzah? Rosh Hashanah? Shouldn't I be in synagogue? Shouldn't I be ushering in the Jewish New Year with the *shofar* or with noisemakers or something? There was always the feeling that I should be doing something that I wasn't doing. Easter? She painted an egg, and she's on her way to heaven! Me, I'm wondering what I'm doing wrong by not doing anything at all!

When Yom Kippur came around, the Day of Atonement, the holiest day in the Jewish year, I especially felt as though I should be doing something that I wasn't doing. Shouldn't I be praying? Shouldn't I be fasting? Shouldn't I be going to synagogue? Shouldn't I be crying? Yes, okay, I should be going to synagogue ... but where? That persistent question. I felt spun around so much when the Jewish holidays came around that I felt as though up was down and down was up and sideways was somewhere in the middle. I didn't know where I was.

For those of you who aren't Jewish (and I sincerely hope there are tens of millions of you reading this book who aren't Jewish, thank you very much), Yom Kippur is like the two-minute warning in football. It's the cry of pencils down on the final exam. In courtroom talk, it's the judge asking members of the jury if they've reached a verdict. Yom Kippur is the foreperson of the jury saying *Yes, your honor, we have reached a verdict. We find this Jew....*

Now how do I describe Yom Kippur to a nice Methodist girl with family roots in East Texas, when I very well know that Yom Kippur is walking down the aisle of a synagogue, staring at fellow Jewish-guilt-sponges in attendance, left and right, and instead of a prison guard saying *Dead man walking*, it's G-d? How do I put that into simple English with a Texas twang?

I took the easy route. I didn't describe Yom Kippur to her at all! I just told her that it was the most serious Jewish holiday of the year, and that I had to go to synagogue. I didn't know what she might have been thinking. I didn't see her painting any eggs, so maybe she knew more than I thought. In reality, at that time, she might have indeed known more about Yom Kippur than I did! So to pretty much pretend we could share this holiday together as part of our connection to each other, we made a decision to find a synagogue we could go to together.

But which one? I still hadn't belonged to any synagogue at that time. Far from it. I wasn't doing anything Jewish beyond Sunday morning bagels. Even if I wanted to belong to a synagogue, I certainly couldn't afford the dues. And besides, even if I could afford to go to a synagogue, to me, those places were most often creepy. If G-d was everywhere, why did I have to go to synagogue to see Him? Or Her? Or It? I didn't know whom I'd be praying to! Couldn't I just go into the kitchen, look up, and ask for forgiveness? I mean, *the kitchen!* What place could be more holy than the place of the coloring of the eggs?

℘ ℭ

Yom Kippur is the day when G-d invites you over to His house—and you'd better be there. I looked in newspapers for ads for synagogues, ones that preferably didn't require tickets. Such synagogues are hard to find. Having to buy tickets for a religious service always made me think that the circus was in town. Which, in many synagogues ... well, we'll possibly get into that at another time.

Just like paying for a class in Judaism, I always thought that synagogues and churches and mosques should be free. How to pay for all these institutions of good, who knows? You'll get no answer to that question here. I will say this, though: poor people and rich people alike are obliged to donate 10% of their incomes to charity. And doing the math: ten percent of a hedge-fund manager's income is a lot more than ten percent of, let's say, a teacher's salary. The teacher might give ten percent but it could never be as much as even, let's say, the half-percent (yes, half-percent) of what a billionaire or millionaire might magnanimously be giving each year. It's the ten percent/half-percent difference. I think we've solved the general charity-giving shortfall right there, but alas, it remains not solved.

The question of how to settle the confusion of the countless number of Jewish people who live through anxiety when the Jewish holidays come around also remains unsolved.

CHAPTER SEVENTEEN

My Yom Kippur – in Church!
Read On....

I noticed an ad in one of the newspapers for a Yom Kippur service: Datadata-yatayata-datayata-blahblah-datadata ... FREE!

Free synagogue service? I'm like a fly in the zapper at a backyard barbecue! I'm the fish that goes for the worm every time! For a place to go to rid myself of guilt for Yom Kippur, this place was priced to attend!

And I was doubly thrilled that I wouldn't have to pay for my girlfriend either. I tried to translate the Yom Kippur synagogue ticket situation into Methodist, for my girlfriend, but that didn't translate either. It's like ordering pigs in a blanket in Yiddish. Order something else. She related paying for a Methodist service to putting coins or bills into a collection plate. To Jews, you pass around any kind of plate in a synagogue, even on Yom Kippur, and the only thing that's going to register is not *How much should I put into the plate?* but: *Awright! There's a buffet!*

℘ ℭ

Yom Kippur was upon us ... well, upon me. (Trust me, Yom Kippur was not upon her at all.) And we had a place to go. Half the load was off my mind, for half of the High Holy Days, that is. And at much less than half the price!

Who cared if the name of the "synagogue" in the ad was something to the extent of: Our Lady of the Something or Other? Temple Beth El would have made me feel a bit more comfortable, but there are a lot of new-age, experimental, reconstructionist, egalitarian, new-fangled Jewish sects that approached Judaism in eye-catching, interesting ways, outreaching to all Jews.... (And some probably very well meaning and pertinent.) But let's call a church a church; I knew in the back of my mind that there weren't any synagogues on the planet that began with *Our Lady! Balabusta*, yes. But *Our Lady?* I think not.

But I was compromising here for the sake of boyfriend-girlfriend peace. And, oh, I'm really sorry to keep bringing this point up, but it was, you know—again—free. And free very often stymies expensive-sounding Jewish synagogue names in favor of affordable-sounding Christian names—you betcha! But what gave me a feeling that I might want to be prepared to pull back the reigns a bit was the fact that the address was on ritzy Park Avenue in New York City. A Yom Kippur service on Park Avenue—a part of Park Avenue with one of the most expensive pieces of real estate in the country, or maybe in the

world—at Our Lady of the Something or Other? For free? I was beginning to get the distinct feeling that it must be, indeed, an extremely
reformed reform synagogue—many times reformed! I immediately
thought that I would gladly pay fifty bucks if they could see their
way clear to maybe changing the name of this place to, well, *nothing!*
Take the "Our Lady" out of the name and give me two tickets to the
place—with no name—where the Yom Kippur service is going to be.

But then I started to think that there was an upside to this Our
Lady of the Something or Other situation: I figured my girlfriend might
have felt a bit more comfortable going to a synagogue starting with the
words *Our Lady* than a synagogue ending with the word *synagogue!*

Ɇ ⚃

A somewhat important point to bring up now would be to mention
that I was bar-mitzvahed at a synagogue called Zion Temple in the
Bronx, on the Grand Concourse and Tremont Ave. It was in my
mind throughout this experience, and was always in my mind when
going to any synagogue.

Remembering that, I quickly rationalized my current circum-
stance away by figuring that I would have a place to go for a Yom
Kippur service; someplace where the cost wouldn't be a prohibitive
and annoying factor, and where my girlfriend would seem somewhat
comfortable in a place called—Our Lady of the—oh my G-d, again,
how was this even possible? Okay, relax, maybe it would be a small
side room of a—oh my G-d—*a church! Okay, don't panic,* I thought.... A
lot of churches give their facilities over to other groups or religions as
a courtesy in a gesture of good will to their fellow men and women. A
beautiful gesture. *Yes, that would be it!* This church was concerned that

Jews could have a place to go to pray on Yom Kippur—that would be cost-effective! Maybe it was Christianity's way of saying, *Here, here's one on us!* I think it might even have been one of the points on the agenda at the *Last Supper!* Where could these disciples go to have a complete, affordable, seven-course meal that wasn't going to break their budget? Yes, this church was doing us Jews a service—well, so to speak.

I was suddenly overcome with something that was usually not associated at all with Yom Kippur; something I would call *a good feeling!*

And So, We Arrived

We got dressed up. We went over to Park Avenue to Our Lady of the, you know, Yom Kippur Service, and we went inside. No tickets, no guest list, no nothin'. I expected nineteen cheap Jews; twenty, including me.... There were five hundred people! If they had sold tickets, the place would have been considered sold out, and they would have made a fortune!

We found two seats with the assistance of an usher, and we sat down and waited for ... something. I looked around. The place was ominous. Statues depicting, oh my G-d, depicting things that were—let me put it this way—not at the Zion Temple in the Bronx.

From what I recall, there was a theater-type stage, making us people in the pews the audience. About ten feet to the right (stage right) of the —rabbi's podium, I guess—(although I hadn't disregarded the notion entirely that *Beelzebub* might be the headliner, and maybe the rabbi was the opening act) was a cello on a stand.... A cello in a Jewish service nowadays would not be so unusual. Many synagogue services have musical instrument accompaniment; quite beautiful, and quite appealing to the communities those synagogues served.

Musical instruments, however, would not be allowed to be played in an Orthodox service on Yom Kippur—or on any Jewish Holiday having the same relative requirements as the Sabbath.

I looked again at some of the statues of martyrs: Saint *this martyr*, Saint *that martyr*. I looked at the statues, I looked at the stage, I looked at my Methodist girlfriend, I looked at the cello, and without even having to Google MapQuest, I got the distinct feeling that I wasn't in Kansas anymore.

I could fathom the cello. I could fathom the religious statues. (Many different approaches to Judaism enable synagogues to be adorned with all kinds of art and sculptures.) I could even fathom that the Yom Kippur service was free! But two out of three of those variables? That concerned me.

Zion Temple didn't have any of those features; least of which was being free! Even though we were always told that Zion Temple was a Conservative temple, it wasn't. The women were elevated in a balcony area, separated from the men, the men swaying to and fro in prayer, on the main level, in movement sometimes known as *shuckling*. But as more commonly known, the men were *davening*. We had all called it a Conservative temple; but thinking back, years later, I realized it was Orthodox. The reasoning, of course, was that if it was called an Orthodox synagogue, only the Orthodox would go there. So they called it Conservative, and it was always packed ... even without a cello. I had gone to Hebrew school there, and was bar-mitzvahed there. But back in (oh, my G-d) church, the service was about to begin. I whispered to my girlfriend that I hoped they would pass around the plate soon. She was very impressed. I was very hungry.

৯০ ০৪

A beautiful woman in a flowing gown approached the cello. Everyone applauded. Church-shmurch, so far this service wasn't bad! My girlfriend, of course, pinched my arm to get my mind off the cello—and its mistress. Next, the "rabbi" entered. I mean, we assumed he was a rabbi. He was wearing a *tallis* (prayer shawl), a *yarmulke*, a designer suit, and he was smiling. So far, he was a rabbi. He walked passed the cello player, hugged her, and took his place at the podium. My girlfriend pinched me again. Let's just say, I wasn't looking at the "rabbi."

The lights dimmed, and the beautiful woman began playing the cello—a solemn, low-pitched melody with the theme of, well, death! And suddenly the beautiful cello player grabbed the bow tightly and sawed out a rousing, up-tempo, high-pitched melody to counter the low-pitched, snail's-paced death knell. Everyone was relieved. We would live!

Up till then it was a cello concert with a beautiful woman playing the cello and a spiffy guy that looked like a rabbi, in a church on Park Avenue, on Yom Kippur. But I really must tell you, in a strange way, *free* was still making up for all of this!

The woman ended her cello piece, everyone applauded, and she looked to the—still not apparent to us what his selected profession was—"rabbi" for the start of the "service." He waited for all the applause to end, looked around at everyone, and then began to speak.

"Won't you please open your pamphlets to page one."

Pamphlets? Pamphlets? I knew the term *siddur* (Jewish prayer book), I knew the term *machzor* (Jewish prayer book for the High Holy Days), but pamphlet? At a Yom Kippur service? The word pamphlet smacked of someone's unreadable book of unpublished poems. But I was there to participate, so I opened my *pamphlet* to page one ... a poem!

"Let us read responsively," the "rabbi" said. "Forgive us, for we know not what we do...."

And we responded, "Forgive us, for we know not what we do."

"The sins of the flesh and the sins of the spirit," he continued ... and on and on and on and on.

And then the beautiful woman played the cello, and we turned to page two. And he read, and we read, and she played the cello, and we hummed, and he read, and she played, and we swayed, and she swayed, and the cello swayed, and he swayed, and he raised his hands high up in the air, and we raised our hands high up in the air, and the beautiful woman raised the cello high up in the air and, I swear—I looked toward the back of the church to see if Elmer Gantry was going to come flying in on his knees! And the *whatever he was* asked us to hold hands. So we all held hands. He asked us to hold hands tighter. So we held hands tighter. The beautiful woman stopped playing the cello, and she clasped both of her hands together. And with his hands held high up to the ceiling, he shouted slogans in English, with Hebrew words carefully thrown in here and there. Before we could figure out what the Hebrew words meant, we were asked to hug the person we were with. Not a problem. And then he asked us to hug the person on the other side of us. Problem. Not only was this man not as attractive as my girlfriend, this man was nowhere near as attractive as the Hunchback of Notre Dame! But I hugged him for the sake of Yom Kippur bliss. And then the beautiful woman with the cello began making music again, and the frenzy of hugs continued as I shoved Quasimodo away from hugging me! I think my girlfriend was delighted. To her, this "service" must have been a *service*.

In the *mosh pit* of hugs and grasps and cello music and Hebrew words, we all heard the name of the person the Christians refer to as the *messiah* hurled to us from the podium—like the moment a proposal is finally unleashed of how many condominium time-shares in Vacationland would we would like them to put us down for!

As everyone continued hugging and smiling and swaying and humming, I stopped doing all these things. I thought back and didn't seem to remember at Zion Temple the name the Christians used to denote G-d's son as generally being any part of the Yom Kippur service. Not that I remembered it as being an integral part of the Rosh Hashanah service either, but I certainly didn't remember it being mentioned on Yom Kippur. Ever.

I suddenly realized that not only weren't we in Kansas anymore, but we had somehow taken the Yellow Brick Road one exit too far and were now heading toward whatever town was one exit past Oz!

℘ ℭ

This service was a service for Jews by Jews with their own ideas of Yom Kippur—and of Judaism! They used the Jewish High Holy Days as an open invitation to entice the wandering. (Please know here, also, that there are some well-meaning Jewish congregations that do use churches to hold services, for lack of their own synagogues or as temporary quarters.) At first look, it would not seem problematic. But, even with those other Jewish congregations, if baseball is played on a basketball court, and basketball played on a baseball diamond, well—you tell me how to keep score.

Everyone continued hugging and smiling—and not objecting—and after reading more words we were finally asked to turn our pages to the closing prayer, which sounded like a selection of greeting card sentiments for the bereaved.

What made this service all so intolerable to me was that it was all so beautiful; like a greeting card—a musical greeting card. A cello-playing, musical greeting card! As a matter of fact, I actually looked on the back of the pamphlet to see what the little numbers were, because I was always told that the first few numbers on the back of a greeting card usually denoted the price. There were no numbers. But there were some words alluding to the name of the person held dear to Christians mentioned in the service.

Apparently, for that Yom Kippur service, that was the price.

℘ ☙

The service ended, the beautiful woman continued playing the cello, the *rabbi/minister/priest/guy* walked to the rear of the church, and we all filed out after him slowly. Congregants were milling around him, quietly thanking him, hugging him; the beautiful woman cello player was still playing the cello, and everybody was happy. A good time was had by all ... on Yom Kippur.

Pamphlets and booklets and magazines and flyers and buttons were on a table for everyone to pick up and take home. Buttons? Yes. Buttons! I can't tell you what was written on the buttons, but it was something to the extent of: Go G-d! I can also tell you that buttons were no part of any Yom Kippur service I had ever remembered, anywhere! As I remembered, with most everyone clutching to life while fasting, if buttons had been part of a Yom Kippur service, we would have eaten them! But at this "service" everyone was grabbing pamphlets and booklets and buttons and candy ... oh yes, candy!

Nobody seemed to mind that this was a quasi-Jewish-Christian Yom Kippur-type service, in a church, with a cello and buttons and saint statues and pamphlets and candy. The adults didn't seem to mind, and the few children who were there certainly didn't mind.

And the Sad Thing Is....

If the adults who were there never experienced a real *Kol Nidre* Yom Kippur service, how would they know this wasn't it? How would they know their grandparents and great-grandparents in places like Russia and Poland and Germany didn't attend Yom Kippur services just like this one? How would they know? Many in the crowd didn't seem to know. And didn't seem to care. They didn't seem to care that this "Jewish" service was different from all other Jewish services.

℘ ℨ

The reason I knew, and possibly others who were there knew, was because I had seen how the Yom Kippur services were conducted at Zion Temple in the Bronx.

It was a temple where there was no cello, and it was a temple where the services were long and detailed; a temple where the Jewish Star of David was prevalent and there wasn't a statue to be had. And it was a temple where the women (during prayers) sat separately from the men out of modesty.

And women sat separately from the men during Yom Kippur services *especially* when men's atonement for transgressions and women's atonement for transgressions were personal matters between men and G-d, and between women and G-d. To pray separated at that time—as our ancestors prayed—in the cities and *shtetels* of Eastern Europe and Western Europe provided an elevated mood to the service that served as a spiritual privacy.

It was the Yom Kippur service where we read from the *machzor* (Jewish prayer book for the *Yom Tovim*–Holidays) about the great sacrifices made by the Jewish-Sage martyrs. It was the Yom Kippur service where we read about the *Kohen Gadol*, the high priest in the ancient temple in Jerusalem, entering the Holy of Holies (the Ark of the Covenant) once a year, on Yom Kippur.

These were—and are—parts of the Yom Kippur prayer service that were, and are, so intense, so personal to each Jew. So we fast, reminded only of the purpose of Yom Kippur: affording us a way to atone for the past year's transgressions. Again, like the archer drawing back the string of the bow: the bow is strung, the arrow put onto the string, the string pulled back, and then at the close of the Yom Kippur service (the *Ne'ilah* Service) all we have to do is let go.

ℰℬ

A line was certainly broken at that gathering in that church that night—Jewish people settling for something other than what is rightfully theirs. It might have seemed insignificant at the time, but it would certainly matter in the long term. Maybe the children who were there would also take their children to an even more unique so-called Yom Kippur service. And one day it might not even be called the Day of Atonement anymore; it might simply be called a show.

I remember as a boy—when I was the same age of those children—sitting in Zion Temple on Yom Kippur, wishing I could be any place else but there.

And there I was so many years later at that some sort of not-Jewish service—on Yom Kippur—knowing that, for myself, as a Jewish person, I should be any place else but there.

CHAPTER EIGHTEEN

Up the Mountain, Choosing a Mitzvah ... Bikur Cholim

When the Jewish-Methodist boyfriend-girlfriend team talked about marriage and children and how to set up a home, they decided not to talk about it. There was nothing to talk about. We went our separate ways. And today, many years later, being in contact very recently, she is herself and I am myself. And neither of us is at a loss. A lesson learned? Try to envision the end result before the beginning. And the other lesson I learned? The more I stay connected to who I am, the less vulnerable I am to those who might try to get me to be who they want me to be. Nothing is as resilient as a strong foundation.

The experiences that led me toward Jewish observance were vast and many. It all adds up. And it all added up. I started to see the big picture;

life as being those marathons I ran. I stopped pretending. Call it a right of passage into adulthood. Call it being true to oneself. Call it responsibility—to oneself and to others. Call it maturing. Call it strength. Call it preparing for the long race, pacing oneself; and call it life.

Several years after that relationship, in 1989, 1990, and thereafter, I started learning about Jewish observance in earnest. I was enjoying it, and I felt very motivated until I had heard that it was desirable for a Jew to choose a *mitzvah* to pursue, one that I could, so to speak, call my own. I was reluctant. It represented commitment. I was nervous about this prospect. I was committed to stand-up comedy. I thought, isn't that a mitzvah? Making people laugh? A mitzvah is thought of as something good a person does. And it is. But it's more than that.... Helping a person to the other side of the street, picking up a piece of litter, pointing out to a person that they dropped their wallet ... these are good deeds; not necessarily mitzvahs. Mitzvahs are connections. Connections to G-d. And they are commandments, not suggestions.

ഗ ന

I attended a series of lectures on mitzvahs, and one that especially caught my attention was *bikur cholim* (visiting the sick). I didn't say it was the one I wanted to do, I just said it caught my attention. As a matter of fact when I learned what bikur cholim was, at that point in my life, I didn't want to do it at all. Visiting the sick on a weekly basis? No thanks. Don't get me wrong, I hope they get better, but I don't think I want to agree to make visits every week. But it stuck in my mind.

The woman presenting the lecture (during the ten days between Rosh Hashanah and Yom Kippur in 1988 at Lincoln Square Synagogue in Manhattan) was a bikur cholim volunteer who was relating her experiences visiting an elderly man in the hospital who had no remaining relatives. She made a commitment to visiting him on a regular basis, and visited him until his death. When I heard that, I wanted to run the other way. That's an adult dose of commitment! I'll visit occasionally, but on a regular basis? Could I do that? Am I ready for that? I answered my own questions: no! But then I remembered, of all the choices of lectures to attend, why I chose to attend this lecture in the first place.

When I was a boy, my father was in the hospital for several days at Montefiore Hospital in the Bronx. As it happened, at that same time, I happened to have been taken to Montefiore with bronchial pneumonia. I was on one floor of the hospital, my father on another. I was there all of two days, and on the second day, when I was feeling much better, I left my room to visit my father. Of course, I didn't tell anyone where I was going. I just left. I found my father's room, and went in to visit. My father was shocked! Of course, my mother didn't tell him I was in the hospital so that it wouldn't upset him, but to a young boy that's not so relevant an issue (especially since I knew nothing about it). After my father got over the initial worry, we had a very comforting visit. (What my father and mother were going to talk about later that day was another story....)

During my visit to my father, I was somehow compelled to visit everyone else in his room as well. There were four beds. My father was motioning for me to come back to his bedside, but I was in the middle of conversations with the other patients. I finally went back to my father's bedside, and after staying with my father for a good long time, I went back to my floor and to my room. My nurse went ballistic. I told her where I had gone, and she told me never to leave the floor again. So I didn't. I wouldn't dare. She was three times my size, and angry! From that time, I couldn't visit patients on other floors so I started visiting patients on my own floor.

When I heard the instruction in the bikur cholim training many years later as to what not to ask a patient, that's how I knew not necessarily to ask the question *How are you feeling* or *How are you getting along.* I remembered that when I asked that question to patients in my father's room, they told me how they were getting along. A simple "fine" or "eh" would have sufficed, but the stories I got (like I was some sort of kid-doctor) ranged from intricate details of their operations—with upper-body scars proudly displayed—to medical terms that some doctors would have to go on sabbaticals to the finest medical institutions in Scandinavia to decipher! I listened, and after the diagnosis, prognosis, and all the other *osises* were expounded upon, I said, "Well, hope you feel better."

It was like saying to Albert Einstein, after he might have explained his Theory of Relativity to me, "Well, you know, best of luck with that, Alby."

In short, I learned not to ask a patient I wasn't related to or a personal friend of how they felt or how they were getting along. The patients I visited were lucky I wasn't contagious. (I was just recovering from pneumonia, remember?) I had a bad coughing spell the first night, and that was it. My mother had heard about my wandering visits in the hospital and she told me to mind my own business. Good motherly advice.

As I was leaving the hospital to go home, the last person I saw was a patient named Johnny. He was a patient in the hospital, but he was always in the lobby greeting people. He was pretty much stationed there in his wheelchair greeting everybody like he was a professional greeter at a Las Vegas hotel. "Welcome to Montefiore Hospital!" he would say.

And then he would go into his routines, kidding about how bad the food was or how difficult it was to find anything in the hospital; and that was his life. I had seen him a few times before when my father was previously at Montefiore. We found out later that Johnny was there pretty much permanently. Before I left the hospital, I asked my mother take me over to him. I couldn't leave the hospital without saying goodbye to Johnny. But it wasn't saying hello or goodbye to each other as much as visiting each other. You see, I was in a wheelchair too, being taken to the front door to be discharged. Johnny was a model bikur cholim volunteer. He made me feel good. He was always smiling, and had a contagious laugh. And of all the things in the hospital that could be contagious, this was something good to catch. I always remembered Johnny. Many years later, when I visited (this time my mother), I looked for Johnny-in-the-lobby (as he was known). Of course, he wasn't there. I stood there looking at "his spot" where he would always sit. I pictured him greeting everybody, smiling, and cheering up just about everybody with whom he came into contact. I missed him. I never knew what illness he had or anything about him other than he was a patient at Montefiore on a long-term basis. I never knew the arrangement, but he was always there.

I went up to the floor where my mother was. And on the same floor was a patient whose son I'd known in the Jewish community, so I visited his father as well. Visiting patients by then was not something out of the ordinary for me; it was the mitzvah I had chosen to do. At that point in my life, with my Jewish life being renewed, as it was, I couldn't simply mind my own business. My mother would have been proud.

ഇറ ☾

Six months after the lecture at Lincoln Square Synagogue I tried bikur cholim, and I've been doing bikur cholim ever since, for over twenty years now. My commitment to visiting patients in the hospital became one of my places in my community. At that time, as a working comedian, I had been removed from that community. I was part of—well, entrenched in—the comedy club community. What went on in my neighborhood community, I thought, had been the community's concern, not mine. I was too busy having fun…. But I eventually got to thinking that having fun was all I was doing. I was somehow awakened by an opportunity to do something worthwhile. I knew I had to follow that opportunity.

In the mundane world, with all the defenses necessary for us to put up for our own protection—and all the stress to put up with—bikur cholim gives me a chance to be kind to people, without worrying if I'm being too vulnerable. Visiting patients allows me to express my compassion for people at least once a week. And it gives me a chance to be an active part of my home community. And it turns out to be a mitzvah as well.

ഇറ ☾

I eventually joined a group from a local synagogue in New York that visits patients at Mount Sinai Hospital in Manhattan. Since performing this mitzvah, I have seen two people die. I had visited them and had gotten to know them on repeated visits. The first person was a woman at Roosevelt Hospital in Manhattan. The other was a man at Mount Sinai who had gone from a regular room to the intensive care unit. He died there. His family was there with him. The woman at Roosevelt Hospital had no one there except the attending nurse and me. I watched the woman take her last breath. I grew up a little that day. Probably a lot. I felt very close to both the man and the woman; not because we had anything in common, we really didn't, but because we were Jewish. And it impressed me how important that was, and is. When one Jew dies, *all Jews mourn*. When one Jew is born, *all Jews rejoice*. We're a people. And anyone or anything that gets in the way of that, gets in the way of not just one of us, but all of us.

℘ ℭ

Bikur cholim, as I've learned, is one of the most important mitzvahs. But it's not for everybody. I learned that when choosing a mitzvah we should choose one that we will want to rush to do. I chose one that, at the time, being entrenched in a comedy club culture, I couldn't imagine doing—much less rushing to do it! But when I finally made the decision to take on this mitzvah, I realized that, as it suited me years ago in my father's hospital room, it suited me now. Each time I was about to do the mitzvah, I did look forward to doing it.... The memory of rushing out of my hospital room and off my floor to visit my father was still with me. It wasn't anything I had to add to myself, it was something already there. And now it was something I wanted and needed to do if I was going to be true to myself.

That lecture I attended about bikur cholim at Lincoln Square Synagogue came full circle. I was now the one who could give a lecture like that. The facts, the circumstances, are so similar. I've seen so many different patients now. And I make my commitment to visit regularly those patients who return to the hospital, and who want me to visit. Each volunteer visitor develops a different rapport with each patient. If two people visit together, one might have a more direct connection to a patient than the other. And on the visit to the next room, that patient might take more to the other visitor or vice-versa. One patient in particular with whom I always visit when she's at Mount Sinai I've known for many years now. I've been to their home (she and her husband's and now their grandchildren's) for a Jewish holiday, and have gone to the wedding of one of the children of another patient's family that I visited also for quite some time.

The two patients I am referring to are both chassidic. But even as part of the bikur cholim group from an Orthodox synagogue, we visit all Jewish patients regardless of affiliation. And we also visit, of course, non-Jewish patients in the room—or if their name sounds Jewish and they turn out not to be. Some are women who are not Jewish, but married to Jewish men. Their last names work wonders for them to get visits from bikur cholim volunteers and it probably works wonders for them to get off work for the Jewish holidays, so mazel tov! Whether Jewish or not, a visit to someone in the hospital is a visit to someone who could probably use a visit. A human being is a human being. I've learned a great deal from visiting non-Jewish patients, whether religious or not. They're almost always appreciative of a visit. The non-Jewish religious patients have a perspective that is quite different than that of some Jewish patients. And their appreciation of having a visit is, not almost, but always very sincere. The similarities in what they talk about in terms of approaching their illness and guidance from their respective religions is quite uncanny. They all sound so Jewish! Some do try to proselytize, but it's always quickly set aside when I try to guide the conversation to things more general. If they get too "religious" on me, they can always expect from me a quick comment on the day's weather! There's no greater equalizer than talking about the day's weather. Many patients ask how the weather is that day anyhow. It's such a popular subject that I'm thinking of suggesting to the United Nations that at their next General Assembly meeting they talk about nothing but the weather!

℘ ℭ

Visits to Jewish patients are divided up into different categories of subject-talk: the weather, the food, and more than I'd like, the various denominations of Jews: Reform, Conservative, Orthodox, Chassidic, Ultra-Orthodox (whatever that is), Reconstructionist (also, whatever that is) etc. (if there is an etc.).

As I've seen, the Jewish patients who fare well with illness in the hospital are the ones who are at ease with themselves, and in many instances, their respective places in Judaism, as the non-Jews are comfortable with their places in their respective religions. It's a pleasure to see. They really rely on their faith to uplift them in their time of illness. And it doesn't seem to be a matter of religious practice. I think, for many Jews, it's more a matter of feeling close to their Jewishness. I have not visited anyone in the hospital who is joyous about their stance against religion. Committed, energetic, forceful, yes, but not joyous.

I have also seen many people dealing well with their illness who are not religious at all. We can all learn from each other. Jews and non-Jews. Religious and non-religious. We cannot judge each other; we can, though, all comfort each other.

ℰℭ ℂℛ

As a Jew, visiting all Jews is a pleasure; but watch out, there can be side effects. And the side effects hit all denominations! The Reform and Conservative Jews almost always ask if I'm from an Orthodox synagogue. Almost always. When I say that we're all Jews regardless of affiliation, many of them seem to not like that answer. They want to know what kind of synagogue I'm from. Some of them think I'm there to ask them for a contribution of money. I don't know if they're scared of me because I'm from an Orthodox synagogue or scared because it may cost them money. Many times I will visit and they will automatically ask where they can send a contribution. I tell them my visit has nothing to do with a contribution of money. Then they think I'm from a synagogue on Mars.

And while Chassidic Jews have much to teach in their coping with illness, they can drive a visitor crazy by asking a million personal questions! While visiting Chassidic Jews I try to point out the nice flowers on their table, and they respond by saying, "Yes, they are nice flowers ... are you married? How many children do you have? What synagogue do you go to? Did you go there today? Did you have a minyan? How many people were there? Did they have a nice kiddush (food after services)? What do you do for a living? Do you rent, do you own? Do you have a co-op?" Visiting some Chassidic or Orthodox Jews can be like walking into an IRS office, standing on a chair and shouting, "I'm here, what up?" (Expect to stay there a while, and be prepared to answer some questions.)

If Reform, Conservative and Orthodox Jews knew how much they have in common in this side-effect-marathon we would, indeed, again be the one people we were at Mount Sinai.

But the side effects that worry me most and that I'm most fearful of are visits to patients who, in conversation, find out that I'm a comedian. As soon as they ask, and as soon as I hear that word comedian come out of my mouth I want to say, "I mean, a plumber!"

Too late. Their next words are always: "Yeah, well, tell me a joke!"

So I try to accommodate with a joke. I tell it, and the patient wheezes and shakes! I look at the nurse; she's smiling, laughing, but apparently not concerned with the patient's—what looks like a mild—tantrum. The patient is all hooked up to tubes and other devices and I'm very happy the joke made the patient laugh, but I don't need a patient's worsening condition on my conscience for the rest of my life because I told a joke that made their tubes shake! I try to severely limit jokes or routines at a patient's bedside. If we have such a rapport where laughs are in the mix to begin with, I can keep it going, but not without reassurance from the patient—over and over again—that laughing is good for them. It usually is. It's worked wonders for some patients through the years who have, on their own, brought laughter into their recovery process. But visitors should take strict cues from the patient before even attempting to bring laughter into the room.

All the denominations of Jews, all the different personalities, the quirks, the stories, the backgrounds ... the side effects. They're all parts of our people.

I don't know whether the two Jewish people I had seen die in hospital were Reform, Conservative, Orthodox, Reconstructionist, or unaffiliated. And I never will.

ℬ ℭ

Choosing my mitzvah was a clear path toward awareness, both inward and outward. It was encouraging to me, on my path, in my pursuit of observance, in a very meaningful way. I had a mitzvah. I was connected. Like a marathon runner hitting "the wall," at some point I stopped running. The next marathon would require more intense, quality training which I looked forward to doing.

It was clear that one of the very positive aspects of my life that I was certainly running away from made me like Jonah with the whale. I wasn't, however, swallowed up by a big fish; although in the lifestyle I was leading....

Be Aware When You Become Aware

Jewish observance is very grounding—a true foundation. It's G-d's commandments of how to live. Choosing life is the commitment. Mitzvahs are getting out there and doing. In the great classic Chassidic work, *Tanya*, authored by the first Lubavitcher Rebbe, Shneur Zalman of Liadi, we learn the concepts of thought, speech, and action. Each is connected, but thought and speech without action are incomplete. To me, bikur cholim is "living observance." To be sure, being connected through prayer is important and studying the laws (*halacha*) of Judaism is important. But action is key: like giving charity to someone who asks, and wishing them well; helping someone rebuild a damaged structure; tutoring students through a troubling subject; visiting the sick; and many other things that help you actively connect with people. Think it first, talk about it next—then do it!

In my training for bikur cholim I learned (according to a reference in *Talmud*, and expounded upon by Maimonedies, the

RaMBaM) that when a person visits someone who is sick, that visitor heals a portion of the illness. Since many vaccines consist of a small part or a weakened or killed portion of a disease-causing microorganism, in this example, visiting patients, helping others, putting others above oneself, giving back to one's community—these are all aspects of building up strength, like a practical vaccine, against an array of maladies. Who knows, maybe one way of looking at Judaism, the Jewish people (or any righteous religion, for those people who are a part of that religion) is seeing its good tenets and teachings as ways of building up immunities against choosing less desirable paths. Something I learned when I started moving on a more productive path toward my real self was that taking tiny steps in that direction was far more beneficial than taking giant leaps in every which direction. Looking back to move forward was, and is, very tough, very personal, and very necessary.

CHAPTER NINETEEN

Be an Angel ... Give Tzedakah

The comfort I felt, the security, the foundation—returning to my Judaism was and is all of that. But, like blasts from the trumpets alerting the troops, the word was out: there's somebody new in the Jewish community—after him! I got on every *tzedakah* (charity) mailing list there ever was.... To give charity. Sweet surrender.

When I first heard the word *tzedakah*, I thought they were talking about the singer Neil Sedaka! I was looking forward to hearing from him! I always liked his songs. But I waited and waited and when I found out that I wouldn't be hearing from Neil Sedaka at all, I was crushed. He was right: breaking up is hard to do!

Being part of a community and being asked to give charity can be a bit imposing. The request letters started coming in.... Please give to this synagogue and please give to that synagogue and please give to this organization and please give to that organization and please give to this Yeshiva and please give to that Yeshiva.... And please give to this person because this one's down on her luck and please give to that person because that one's down on his luck, and please give to this deserving couple because this deserving couple has twelve kids and the oldest one's getting married and the son's being bar-mitzvahed and they need a new washing machine and the daughter's getting married and she needs to buy a hat and her fiancé's out of work and his teeth need a cleaning.... So I gave! (And still nothing from Neil Sedaka.)

Then the letters really started streaming in from synagogues, from organizations, from the needy, the friendly, the Yeshivas: Can you double your last gift to us? Can you triple it? Can you make it a monthly gift? Can you at least match the gift you gave us last time? Can you match the gift you gave to us before the one you gave us last time? Can you save us the cost of postage by putting a postage stamp on the envelope when you send us your gift? Can you put us in your will? Can you remember us in your estate? Can you tell us how old you are? Do you exercise regularly? Can you tell us how you feel? Do you eat a lot of Mrs. Lot Sandwiches? Can you consider increasing the amount you'd be donating to us in your will? Can we have your car? No, seriously, can you donate your car to us? We'll come pick it up; you don't have to do a thing! And if you put a stamp on the envelope when you respond to us to let us know where we can pick up the car, that's an added gift to us.... And can you leave the car with a full tank of gas?

I was inundated! I sent them eighteen dollars and a stamp. And many times, I sent more. But only one stamp per customer.

The different levels of giving and gradations of gifts fascinated me. In the Jewish community, charity is customarily given in denominations of eighteen dollars (the numerical equivalent of *chai*—the Hebrew word for life). Every gift denomination is given a title. The top title, to denote the very greatest gift, is very often called: *Benefactor*. The usual contribution for this honor is very often called fifty thousand dollars. (It, of course, varies according to the function or the appeal, but fifty thousand dollars is a safe Benefactor level.)

They usually had to make up a non-existent level for me. I once gave seven dollars. I believe in most Jewish circles that's known as the *Shlump* level (pronounced *shlump*)! This level is not even represented as a box to check on the return card in the envelope. To them, the figure is so minuscule that they ask the shlump to write in the amount! They don't want to touch it! (They're embarrassed to even ask the printer to make a little box that the shlump can check denoting a seven-dollar donation!) I was so intimidated that, after that, I gave at least eighteen dollars every time. In one return envelope, I was shocked, the card actually did have a box to check for an eighteen-dollar donation.... Contributors who checked this box were actually, in this case, given the title: *Angel*. I went from being a Shlump to being an Angel for eleven dollars!

Along with Angels and Benefactors, some synagogues cleverly use *synagogue themes* to denote the various levels of giving. Here are some levels for the more desperate shuls: *The rabbi's confidant*: five thousand dollars; *Close friend of the rabbi's confidant*: one thousand dollars; *Friend of the brother-in-law of the rabbi's confidant*: two hundred and fifty dollars; *Friend of the guy who cleans up after the kiddush:* thirty-six dollars; *Shlump:* seven dollars.

The donation levels can also go the other way too, by starting with very prestigious levels for the lesser donations, and ending up somewhere in the tzedakah ionosphere for the largest donations.... The very lowest level in this case being *Supreme Holy Jew of the Century:* eighteen dollars. (I can't tell you what title thirty-six dollars gets you— all I can say is that it makes Moses look like, well, a shlump!)

If you'd like to consider donating to your local synagogue, please, don't get discouraged, get your checkbook out and pick one of these available honored contribution possibilities: *Synagogue Building Builder, Backyard Landscape and Mikvah Builder; Ritual Pool; Ritularium; Front Lawn Landscape, Mikvah and Building Builder; Building, Landscape with a fountain, Heated Pool, Mikvah, Kitchen, Library and Stained-Glass-Windows Builder; Towels for the Mikvah Provider, Unlimited Soap for the Mikvah and a Large Box of Yarmulkes Donator, Building Extension Builder, Porch Builder, Rooftop-Hockey-Rink-Builder, Ping-Pong Tables Donator; Regular Kitchen, Passover Kitchen, Kitchen on the Third Floor That Nobody Uses Giver; Full College Library with X-Box Room ... and Plasma TV and Computer Rooms.* If you really need a nice tax write-off, consider sponsoring the ultimate in synagogue indulgence that surprisingly very few synagogues have: *A Full-Time Professional Lifeguard for the Mikvah!* And for the very highest donation to any synagogue, your offering will be duly noted with: *A Seat Near the Rabbi at the Annual Fundraising Banquet, a Gold Page in the Dinner Program—* and what will make you the envy of the community—a truly tear-rendering honor, where chicken is the only choice at the annual banquet other than fish or a vegetable plate—your superior donation will make you the recipient of the much ballyhooed *Beef Option* presentation!

And, of course, the very highest, highest, highest, superior title that can be bestowed upon a congregant to denote the most staggering synagogue contribution, reflecting the most generous and magnanimous of financial proportions, your donation will be accepted with the most gracious and coveted *It's Okay For You to Talk in Shul* level!

Oh, don't worry, there's always more when giving is concerned; for you billionaires, you can give five hundred thousand to an organization that's trying to raise a hundred and twenty million for their new building complex, and they'll send you back a thank-you note reading: Thank you, we appreciate your most generous five-hundred-thousand-dollar donation to our building fund. We take pride in acknowledging you as one of our dear *Unemployed Congregants!*

Dare to give anything less than one hundred thousand dollars to a fundraiser like this and, get ready, you can expect the thank you note to begin with: *Dear Shlump....* But don't feel demeaned. You can always elevate your under hundred-thousand-dollar donation by putting a stamp on the envelope! It raises you to the donation level of *Shlump with a Stamp!*

ℰℛ

I would often wind up with a stack of appeal envelopes, which made my desk look like I was living at the Post Office. Which would have been very convenient since I would never have had to add a stamp!

I couldn't possibly give to everyone. Or even near that. So I would pick and choose regular charities and occasionally new ones. Every time I gave, I felt good. Which probably irked some of the organizations that were waiting for me to leave the planet, in order for my will to kick in. But these organizations shouldn't despair—everyone has to go sometime. And they can take great estate-donation-comfort in the fact that even though I always try to stay in good shape, I do occasionally order a Mrs. Lot'O Sandwich with extra meat ... and a pickle!

So feel free to ask for that estate donation in the future.... Hopefully the very distant future! And feel good—because whenever the recipients of contributions in my will are revealed, you'll be very comforted to know that I've already made specific arrangements for my executor to put stamps on all the envelopes!

So Is There a G-d or Isn't There?

Uh, oh. I was hoping this question wouldn't come up!

My answer? Yes, there is a G-d. Most certainly.

Can I prove it? No. Most certainly.

Do I believe it? Yes. Most definitely.

Is G-d an old man with a white beard somewhere in the sky?

Okay, you know, that's a good question. No, I don't believe that G-d is an old man (or an old woman) with a white beard somewhere in the sky. But let me get back to you on that, just to cover myself. Not in this lifetime, you understand, but let me get back to you on that.

By the way, that's what people who don't believe in G-d and I have in common: we both don't believe that G-d is an old man or an old woman with a white beard somewhere in the sky. (And sometimes I think that that's the only image of G-d that people who don't believe in G-d don't believe in.)

Do I believe in love?

Well, yes.

Can I prove that love exists?

Well, no.

If someone who is in love sends flowers and candy to the one he or she is in love with, isn't that proof of love?

Boy, wouldn't that be nice!

Is a rose beautiful?

Yes.

Can I prove that a rose is beautiful?

No.... I mean, it looks beautiful ... to me. I think it must look beautiful to most others. But can I prove that it's beautiful? Well, no. How would I prove that? Is there a lab test that proves definitively that a rose is beautiful?

Is a weed ugly?

Yes.

But now I bet a weed is probably beautiful to some people. But, I assure you, send a weed to somebody you love because you think a weed is as beautiful as a rose, and you can start making dinner reservations for one. And I think I can prove that!

Does emotional pain exist?

Yes.

Prove it.

I can't. I can only show you the love letters ... and the dinner receipts for one.

The levels of a person's soul may exist or not exist, and we have no way on earth of proving any of it! How can we prove a soul exists? How can we prove what a soul is? If a tree falls in the forest, does it make a sound? Yes, it has to. If something falls, it makes a sound. If we don't hear it, then did it, indeed, make a sound? Look, I don't know; I try not to go into the forest in the first place; it's too buggy.... So whether a tree falls in the forest or not, I'm the wrong one to ask; I'm rarely there.

Do bugs exist?

Oh yes.

Where do bugs come from?

Uh ... the forest?

Where does the forest come from?

Uh ... the earth?

Where does the earth come from?

You know, I didn't know we were going to have a test today! This really isn't fair.

Does belief exist?

I don't know....

Can we prove that belief exists?

I want to go home now!

You can't go home just yet. You have to finish what you started.

Look, all I know is that people who don't believe in G-d don't have a real teaching, a structure, a heritage. They might very well believe in a goodness they embrace; and I'm certain many people who don't believe in G-d do embrace goodness. Most certainly. They might not call it a belief in G-d, but it just might very well be from G-d's hand. Can I prove it? No, not at all.

All I'm saying is that I guess people who believe in G-d have that certain something, that essence of belief, that spirit that keeps the people who believe in G-d together, and certainly together as a people. And from there, they can build. They have a sturdy foundation, as a people; a sturdy foundation that is both physical and spiritual. People who don't believe in G-d might very well derive benefits from G-d, but they don't believe those benefits come from G-d. And so they freely relinquish their right to call upon G-d. It's like being given a gift ... and not opening it.

I gotta go now. I need a week in the forest!

And now, back to the book....

CHAPTER TWENTY

Please Pass On the Pickles, Please

When I felt a little more secure in my learning and in my performance of the rituals of observance, among them being: putting on *tefillin* every weekday morning, keeping kosher again (now inside the house and out), observing the Sabbath, etc., I thought back to some frustrating things that I'd been grappling with for some years. I was observant now, so I looked at things a little differently and felt like I wanted to question some things I had taken for granted that had been ingrained in me, like the notion that Jews keep kosher for health reasons. Keeping kosher has little to do with health reasons; physical health, that is. There is little healthy about *stuffed derma*! I am certain that very few kosher nutritionists are advising people that as long as it's kosher, eat as much stuffed derma as you like.

Without describing exactly what stuffed derma is, suffice it to say that it's best known as *kishka*! And, for the sake of decency, without describing exactly what kishka is, suffice it to say that if you eat kishka, you'll be stuffing *your* kishkas—oh very well, the insides of your stomach—with stuff that originally got stuffed into an animal's kishkas, which gave the stuff the name kishka to begin with! And to add insult to kishka injury, this delicious kosher side dish is usually served with a thick slab of kosher meat that usually has a saturated fat content in the relative vicinity of whale blubber.

So let's keep away from the kishka plate and move on to another Jewish dietary delicacy: chopped liver. What could be more kosher than chopped liver? Well, if it's kosher ... nothing. And just as a casual thought, the cholesterol it's loaded with is kosher as well.... Not to mention the saturated fat contained in the mix, which, by the way, and so sorry for harping on this point—is also kosher. In this case, liver, chopped or not, is very tasty, very kosher, and as we've become well aware of in recent years, somewhat unhealthy. Add the salt, the eggs, the fried onions, the chicken fat, and it still remains kosher—but gets even less healthy.

And as long as we're using chicken fat as the binder—is it kosher? If it's from a kosher chicken, of course it is. Is it healthy? Uh, not really. Why? Because it's fat! From a chicken! It's not as unhealthy as fat from, let's say, kosher *beef flanken*! But it is, nevertheless, not that healthy anyhow.

Why we think fat from a chicken, just because it's kosher, would be healthy, defies all logic. And if chickens had the ability to reason, I'm sure they too would agree. But chickens don't apparently have the ability to reason or I'm sure they would have formed some sort of chicken union long ago. Kosher chickens of the world, unite.

Hold on here.... Let's go back a bit. Did I say kosher chicken fat is healthier than kosher beef flanken fat?

I did. And I'll tell you why: because I think sharing washcloths in a leper colony might be healthier than eating beef flanken fat! And why? Because of the way we cook it! If we would, let's say, broil the flanken, that would cut down on the amount of fat we'd actually be eating. But we don't broil it! We boil it ..! *We boil it!* Can you imagine? Boiling a piece of meat? The fat stays put! Period. I mean, where can it go? The fat looks around, sees the hot water, gets so discouraged that it gives up without even putting up a fight. At least in the four-hundred-degree broiler the fat kicks and screams, dukes it out with the red-hot roaster, breaks into a sweat, and dissolves into *goo* on the fat-catcher broiler-tray, never to be heard from again! And that's the way to do it. Send in your best fighter: the fat-sizzling broiler. But we don't! We look on the bench to see what's available to most effectively cook this fatty hunk'o fatty meat, and we make the decision to send in boiling water! It's astounding; we've actually found a way to make one of the fattiest beef dishes known to humankind even fattier!

Boiled kosher beef flanken: lose the taste, keep the fat.

ഇ ൽ

Now let's stop fooling around and get down to some vital kosher issues here.... Let's talk about some of the strange parts of kosher animals we seem to thrive on, like tongue. Is it kosher? If it's from a cow that's been slaughtered according to kosher law, it is. Is it a tongue? Yes! I understand a wonderfully clean and humanely slaughtered cow leaving behind a tongue—but do we have to eat it? Again ... it's a tongue! I don't think the Torah specifically forbids eating a cow's tongue because at Mount Sinai it probably wasn't even thought of as a possibility!

Which brings us to the non-option of all non-options of kosher dishes: liverwurst! The suggestion of how healthy this kosher meat dish is right there in its name: liver—the oatmeal of the blood stream! And: *wurst*! Without even bothering to find out what the word wurst means, I'm just going to assume that it actually does mean *worst*! I always thought that whoever named this food wanted to name it *liver-best*, but in good conscience couldn't!

℘ ℭ

Okay, here we are ... we've finally arrived at the kosher pickle department. (You knew it was coming.) Okay, take off your shoes, set a spell ... let's see what we've got here.

Kosher pickles.... Now, who doesn't enjoy a nice kosher pickle with a sandwich? You want me to tell you who? People who like liverwurst, that's who. I tell you, these people need to be investigated.

But let's let those people languish in their own *wurst* misery as we explore the endless qualities of the kosher pickle: the salt-laden, brine-drenched cucumber of the accompaniment family! Is it kosher? If it's prepared as such, of course. Is it healthy? Well, now that depends on how much latitude you give to the term *healthy*. If you think too much salt in your diet leading to bloating, high blood pressure, and poor health in general is considered healthy, well, then yes, it's healthy! Are pickles considered too salty? Okay, once again, let's put it this way: when Lot's wife looked back at Sodom and Gomorra, I think G-d might have given her the option of being turned into a Pillar of Salt *or* a Pickle of Salt! She chose Pillar of Salt. Why? Because it's less salty!

ℰꙅ ൠ

I'm sorry to be the bearer of unhappy news, but apparently, the only thing physically healthy about the *mitzvah* of keeping kosher is that we're discouraged from ordering a hot fudge ice cream sundae after eating a combination of pastrami, salami, brisket, bologna, turkey, and corned beef hero—most commonly known, by the way, in many delicatessens, as the *Mrs. Lot'O Sandwich!* (The turkey is thrown in there as a way of introducing lean kosher meats into our diets—if we can stand it.) It all looks beautiful on the plate, but the only unhealthy part is really what *we* choose to eat.

And to show you how easy it is, and how much fun it can be to keep kosher, go ahead, you can even have that hot fudge sundae after the Mrs. Lot meat factory sandwich after all! The "Kosher Institute" (not even close to being the name of a real institute) has painstakingly developed *parve* (neither meat nor dairy) frozen soy bean curd that looks and tastes just as good as real dairy ice cream.... (The institute might not be real, but these parve products are!) And top it off with some parve hot fudge or some parve marshmallow sauce and you're not only eating a yum-yum tasty kosher treat, but it's absolutely all right to eat it right after eating the *Mrs. Lot'O Sandwich meatsa-meatsa* extravaganza! It's guaranteed delicious—and a guaranteed 125 over 613 on your next blood pressure test!

ℰꙅ ൠ

Why can't we Jews stop kidding ourselves? We think eating kosher foods will keep us healthy because we're commanded to refrain from putting a wide chunk of hard, melted kosher cheese on a fat-laden, grease-dripping kosher hamburger! *Why*, we tell ourselves, *that probably cuts out half the fat!* Yeah, like eating one quart of ice cream is less fattening than eating two quarts of ice cream!

℘ ☙

I've seen more rotund Jewish people chowing down on more gobs of unhealthy kosher food than some larger wrestlers at the *All You Can Eat Steak Circus* after a two-out-of-three tag team wrestling match!

It's a myth! Plain and simple. Eating a lot of unhealthy food, even if it's kosher, will not make you healthy. It will make you fat!

And at Passover time it will make you crazy too. Passover is the time when we eat only those foods that are specifically kosher for Passover. The main food that we're commanded to eat, of course, is matzah: called the *bread of affliction*; a well-deserved title. Because even if the Jews didn't have to eat matzah when they left Egypt, this flat flour and water concoction would still have to be termed the bread of affliction as a general warning. Folks, this is not bread that, well, now how can I put it? This is not bread that *moves easily*.

Oh, the Jews leaving Egypt might have carried the matzah on their shoulders easily, but once it got into their stomachs—it wasn't going anywhere! And *they* weren't going anywhere! I happen to think that's what kept the Jews in the desert for forty years. If they could have gotten even a minute amount of fiber in their diets I think they could have made the trip to Israel in about ten days.

No Kidding; Be Conscious First, Eat Second

Eating kosher food will not make you any healthier than eating any other food. What eating kosher food *will* do is make you think. Think before you eat. And you will be doing something that G-d has commanded the Jewish people to do. If you eat only certain foods because those foods are kosher, you will surely think before eating those foods. And if you separate foods because of content—you must think before doing that. If you're thinking about the contents of kosher foods, you will be more likely to recognize healthy contents. There are plenty of healthy kosher foods. Plenty.

If you choose to say blessings before and after eating kosher food, you must think in order to do that too. And if you think before you eat, it will automatically raise your awareness and self control, not only in what you eat—but in everything you do.

℘ ☙

Certain blessings (*brachas*) are said before and after eating kosher food. Saying these blessings for non-kosher foods is not necessary, and it's not done. Anyone can thank G-d for the food they're about to eat, and that's a beautiful thing to do. But Jewish people have particular blessings that are said before eating each of the different kinds of foods—and that's a beautiful thing too.

Being thankful for food is universal. However, the Jewish ways of eating and giving recognition of certain foods are uniquely Jewish ways. As much work as it is—and it is work; time-consuming and cumbersome at times—in the long run we are fortunate to have a unique G-dly commandment to live according to kosher dietary laws. I've found in my own observance that the time it takes to be conscious of these laws, and to incorporate these ways into my life, elevates my life.... A life that is now more grounded in purpose.

ℰ ℭ

Many people think that a certain food becomes kosher because it is *blessed by a rabbi*. This is merely a myth. In reality, food becomes kosher by fitting into the parameters of foods that are kosher according to Jewish law. The only food a rabbi blesses is the food that rabbi is about to eat! If a food is kosher, then we can bless our own food. And in the grand scope of things, if taking time to think before we eat seems to be too much trouble, think about how much trouble we might be in if we don't take that time.

Every Jewish person can incorporate these ways into his or her life. It adds a certain purpose, a spirit, an elevated consciousness to life when you eat kosher food. After all, it's said *we are what we eat*. In a way, blessing our food gives the food life before and after it's eaten. And the food gives us life.

That, in itself, is what's healthy about eating kosher—body and soul.

CHAPTER TWENTY-ONE

A Jewish Way, For Everything ... A Guide

My giving, my observance, my learning, my real joy in knowing that the good times I had now have good, lasting effects, all added up in my return to myself and control of myself.

Vitamins add nutrients to the body. It's rather common knowledge that if taken in a timely manor, and in proper doses, vitamins can be a factor in good health. Many people take a multi-vitamin every day. Many take vitamins for all sorts of purposes. Some take too many, some take too little, some take vitamins once in a while and some don't take any at all. Adding vitamins and nutrients to the diet for a good effect has become a way of life for many people. They start the day with a regimen of vitamin pills, ointments for the skin, liquid solutions to drink, odd concoctions, tea-leaf remedies, boiled Chinese root mixes and who knows what else. They cannot exist, it seems, without their body's intake regimen.

If a vitamin is missed one day, will it have a negative affect on a person's body? If it's prescribed by a doctor or other health professional, it might. If not prescribed, probably not. If a vitamin (not prescribed) is missed for a week, will it have a detrimental affect? Possibly. If it's missed for a very long period of time, will it have a harsh affect? Maybe. Does the body rely on vitamins to exist? Oh yes. If all vitamins, from supplements and foods, are eliminated from a diet, can the body exist? Oh no. If all *nutrients* of a person's soul are taken away, can that person's soul exist? Interestingly enough, yes—but at a loss. A severe loss. Will the person feel it as a loss? Interestingly enough, not necessarily. Can a person exist without nurturing his or her soul? Unfortunately, yes. Is it better to nurture one's soul than to not nurture it? Most definitely.

Okay, how then does one nurture one's soul? I'm glad I asked.... There are a myriad of ways to nurture a soul. Which is best? Who knows. And can these ways be guaranteed to nurture the soul? Guaranteed? Who knows.

℘ ℭ

All religions, disciplines, gurus, motivators, charlatans, television evangelists, well-meaning Public Access TV programs, not-so-well-meaning Public Access TV programs, quacks, psychos, resident institutional day-room orators, and the list goes on and on of people and entities, all have something to say about the soul.

Of course, all noted religions have their respective thoughts. It's what religion is about: the spiritual approach to life based on specific beliefs. There are probably thousands of other ways to put it, but I'm pretty sure that's close to one of the ways. Judaism, as one of the noted religions on earth, is right up there in its teachings.

Judaism addresses ways to nurture the neshama, which can lead to a sense of well-being. And not only well-being, but purpose. Such ways as doing unto others as you would have others do unto you; thinking before eating; thinking about what to eat; thinking about what not to eat; what to say (as in blessings) before eating and what to say after eating are some purposeful teachings to think about. What days to work. What day to rest. What days to celebrate. What days to mourn. What to learn. What to avoid. How to behave. Remedies for misbehaving. A day when it's all right to misbehave (somewhat)—Purim. And how the Jewish way, on that day, to misbehave wildly (somewhat!) can have an elevating affect.... Yes, the neshama runs deep.

Most people live their lives on the surface, never acknowledging that there is another life just inside the surface, and way deeper than that. Most people are reluctant or afraid to visit there, possibly because it runs so deep. It is, indeed, easier to stay put than to travel. But once there, it opens up a whole new dimension of comfort, knowledge, remembrances ... and an infinite number of life-sustaining feelings and knowledge that make a life, well, a life!

Using It

In acting there is a basic tenet of what to do when something goes wrong on stage: use it—incorporate it into the action in a positive way, and move on with the scene and the play. Since everything in Judaism can be related to everyday life, the concept of *using it* can be learned from, and used.

One of the most disruptive events in a person's life is the passing of a loved one. And much more so: the passing of a close family member. Models in everyday life suggest that we use a negative event for a positive effect. Judaism shows us *how* to use it. And meeting, facing, dealing with the reality (as in this instance) of the death of a close family member is an integral part of Jewish observance.

If hugging a loved one always nurtured the soul, then what do we do when that hug, that *vitamin*, that *nutrient* of the neshama is gone? What to do.... In Judaism the loss of a loved one, affecting the soul of the living, is addressed most definitely and in much depth. The neshama is hurt. It's damaged. Like an illness of the body, the soul becomes sick; sick from its loss. And that illness has to be dealt with for it to heal. The Jewish way of facing it is systematic, logical, and comforting. Without it, the soul remains hurt and in extreme disarray and discomfort. An excellent book that addresses this matter (and the many procedures in coping with a loss) is *The Jewish Way in Death and Mourning* by Maurice Lamm.

When a person is ill, that person goes to a doctor. When a person's soul becomes ill, that person can go to a loved one, a friend, a spiritual advisor, or whatever other person or entity that person sees fit to consult with or to be with. When a Jew's neshama is hurt or ill, a Jew can go to all of the above—and also to the centuries of laws and teachings of Torah and its Sages. A competent rabbi will know where to look and how to advise. If a loss is from the death of a close family member there are specific ways to approach the healing process. One of the ways I'll address here is something called *the Kaddish*.

ℰↃ Ↄℛ

The Kaddish is commonly known as a prayer for the deceased. And it is. But it serves many functions. It's a prayer to remember the deceased, yes, but it's a prayer very much also for the living; a prayer for linking the generations; a prayer of continuance; a prayer to bring personal peace.

In Judaism the Kaddish is a prayer that is *prescribed* three times a day. The *prescription* is written (so to speak) and brought to a minyan (a quorum of ten Jewish men), and the prescription is filled—and taken right then and there. By reciting the Mourner's Kaddish at the appropriate times in the service, the emotional pain of losing a specific family member, a loved one, is addressed.

There are many laws of bereavement and of the Kaddish; for whom Kaddish is said, for how long, etc. Traditionally (and according to Jewish law), sons are required to say the Mourner's Kaddish for the mother and the father. (There are other instances also: Mourner's Kaddish to be said for a brother, a sister, a wife, and others, which will not be addressed here.)

ℰↃ Ↄℛ

When my mother passed away in 1999, the emotional stress and sadness and confusion associated with the death of a parent led me around in circles. I didn't know where to begin the process of the many details involved in the death of a family member. I remembered my father's death and funeral, but I hadn't been part of the planning. And I wasn't yet observant. With my mother's passing, I learned about the Jewish way of honoring a parent in death and how to proceed. It was such a comfort; an inspiration.

The immediate time after a death is, of course, the most excruciating, exhausting; physically and emotionally. In Judaism, the first seven days are called the *shiva* period. (The Sabbath or a Jewish Holiday break the shiva period, but that is a matter to learn separately.) "Sitting" *shiva* is like an intense painkiller prescribed right after an operation or period of extreme pain. If there was such a thing as a *Judaica Drug Store*, sitting shiva would be like fulfilling a prescription for a bottle of Percoset! Take it for seven days and, while you're taking it, take some Codeine also! Three times a day (like saying the Kaddish) just sit in the house on a hard bench and let friends and family come into the house to sit with you and give you words of comfort, and you should be okay. If the pain gets worse, call a rabbi and get a *prescription* for some Psalms to read. (I don't know what prescribed drug to relate that to, but I'm sure there is one.)

As all this is going on, the days go by. The emotional pain is supposed to ease somewhat. When the shiva period is over, a walk is taken around the block, and the next phase of the emotional healing begins: the *Sheloshim*. The Sheloshim is a period of thirty days. (The bottle of Percoset is empty, but the Codeine is still to be taken....) Three times a day, continue the Mourner's Kaddish.

A beard starts to grow during the *shiva* period and continues on to the thirty-day Sheloshim. I wished there was a prescribed drug for that landscape growing on me! On others it looks distinguished, purposeful, manly, rugged. On me it looked itchy. I never scratched my face so much in my entire life. I felt like I had a nest of pheasants living in there!

At the conclusion of the Sheloshim, amazingly the Codeine—sorry, I mean the Kaddish—was working. (On me, the beard wasn't.) As the days and weeks passed by I felt more relaxed, more focused, more myself. I actually looked forward to reciting the Kaddish three times a day. I was hooked. I was *addicted*. It was working. It was like a place to go to three times a day for comfort. And in a sense, it was very much like being able to re-visit my mother's memory, three times a day.

During this time period of saying Kaddish, the abruptness of death and its affect becomes dissipated. It becomes not abrupt anymore, but gradual—gradually fading into the past. As the abruptness fades, the emotional strength returns. And the Codeine can be replaced with an over-the-counter drug like ibuprofen.... Also three times a day. And then, after eleven months, no drug—no recitation of Kaddish—is needed. The spiritual loss of the loved one is fading more into the past, and the immediate emotional memories, the pain of the death of the mother or father (or another) fades into the past as well. The pain is replaced with loving remembrance and understanding. If I'd had to face all of it with my own emotional devices, I likely would have been emotionally scarred, instead of spiritually enriched. I would have simply self-medicated myself with ways to confront a parent's death—with, probably, confusing, destructive, and long-lasting consequences. I simply would have been a mass of guilt and anger and frustration. I wouldn't have known what to do, how to go about it in an uplifting way or how to grieve in a purposeful way. I would have just been on my own to do whatever I could do to cope with the loss in my own way, whatever way that would have been. And my frustrations and grief about my mother would have continued on and on, probably forever if there hadn't been a healing way to put a clear break, and a bridge, in between my mother's death and the future. The loss of my mother made me stronger and more responsible and more loving. Not only more loving for my mother, but more loving in general.

One of the reasons I mention my mother's death at all is because I had always had a very strained relationship with my mother. But my Jewish observance brought me closer to my mother in the remaining several years of her life. The bond of Judaism was and is stronger than peoples' differences. Infinitely stronger, thank G-d. Whereas my mother's memory and memories were indeed fading, words sometimes were replaced with Jewish songs she remembered. The melodies and lyrics she remembered vividly. I was amazed. A life of songs emerged, to help my mother communicate from the confusion of words. Jewish memories were brought to the forefront in song and even in the Yiddish language! Something very strong was there. It was a power. Loss of memory was one thing, but this force was something else. It pushed its way forward. Of course, sadly, parts of my mother's life, her past, and her present were very much being erased. But my mother's Judaism, her current place in being part of the Jewish people, was very much there. Incredibly so. A Jewish woman, in a most difficult time, was being peacefully comforted by singing Jewish songs she remembered happily. My mother seemed to have something stronger, even more important, than words of comfort each of us would try to convey. Guiding her on her continuing journey was something more profound. It was something else.

ℰℒ ℭℛ

Each year I remember my mother and my father, and honor their memories—their lives, their being a part of me—by reciting the Kaddish, three times a day on their respective *yahrzeits* (the day of a

Jewish person's death, once a year on the Hebrew calendar). I look forward to reciting the Kaddish each year. I like to feel as though my mother and father can somehow hear me. And I picture them smiling—as I do remember each of their smiles. Each time I attend the *yizkor* service in synagogue (four times a year) and say the passage for each of my parents, I remember something about them....

I remember my mother standing in front of our apartment house on the Grand Concourse off Burnside Avenue, dressed up and carrying her long-strapped pocketbook at her side; my father in a snapshot of him standing in a mountain snow scene in upstate New York, wearing almost knee-length boots with his fisted hands placed on either side of his waist (an identical snapshot for which I later purposely posed in a snow scene myself). After I picture them each in those ways, I see my parents both dancing the waltz they would dance at weddings and bar mitzvahs: the Wedding Waltz.... "Oh, how we danced on the night we were wed...."

My parents were married at a famous kosher restaurant, on 38th Street near Broadway in Manhattan, called Lou G. Siegel's. It was a very common place for Jews of that generation to have their wedding receptions. I once went into Lou G. Siegel's restaurant (luckily right before it closed several years ago), and asked them where a wedding might have been held many years before. I was shown the room. It looked like it hadn't changed since then, and I stood there and pictured my parents dancing the Wedding Waltz. I took the picture in (not with any device, mind you), and left very quickly. The picture is with me forever.

I always feel as though my parents' neshamas are very much alive, along with the neshamas of the generations of my family going back to the journey of the Jewish people out of Egypt. And reciting the Kaddish brings them all back.

The Kaddish is one prescription, one powerful easer of pain that I never would have filled if I hadn't started learning about my Judaism again. A powerful lesson.

The Kaddish. It's not a painkiller at all. It's a prayer that uses the pain and transforms it into something nourishing.

With all the talk about drugs and vitamins and nutrients in our lives, you would think we could never derive the benefits of each without taking a single one of them. The positive after-effects of incorporating some of the other nutrients into our lives, nutrients of the neshama, G-d willing, miraculously, can last a lifetime—and more.

CHAPTER TWENTY-TWO

What's In a Door

Choosing a mitzvah, *learning about kosher again,* learning the prayer services, meeting new friends, getting strange looks from old friends, learning, always learning—and growing, always growing—was all mind-boggling. Becoming observant. Working as a comedian. Stopping work on Friday nights. I was on a fiery path in everything I was doing. But I tell you, I felt like I was driving a used Ford *Mishigas* eighteen miles an hour in the left-hand speed-lane with all four blinkers on and my chin to the steering wheel. Being new to navigating through Jewish observance is one trip AAA simply does not have a *Triptik* for. You know—yet.

Eventually, I found myself on the right road, moving forward, getting somewhere. People were looking at me, I was going the right way, I had a renewed license, people were passing me by ... and I can't think of any more driving references. Oh yes, one more: the last exit on the highway each week was Shabbos. And *now* that concludes all the driving references.

Almost every Shabbat I was able to spend with people. Fellow Jews. But occasionally I was alone. Being alone on Shabbos could be like being at the Grand Canyon and looking the other way.

I started going to shul every Friday night. It added a dimension to my life that was, and I couldn't explain it, somehow missing. I had spent every Friday night for many years in comedy clubs. Being in comedy clubs added an exciting dimension to my life that I also missed. But in a short time I realized that spending time in comedy clubs—that exciting dimension—those industry nights at the hot spots in New York and Los Angeles, and the nights everywhere else—proved to be nothing more than paper fires. But I stayed. I didn't leave those hot nights behind completely, some of them led to very lucrative work ... I just added something more to the fires.

ℴ ℙ

I met people every week who invited me to their homes for Shabbat dinner or lunch. I got many invitations, always. Anyone who is Jewish and who shows a desire to learn about Shabbat will most definitely be received warmly by fellow Jews and be invited very often to Shabbat lunches and dinners. Many times I was out of town for work. And even though (in the beginning) I'd work on Friday nights at the comedy clubs, I would stay with a family Friday night, go to synagogue, have Shabbos dinner with them, walk to the comedy club (if it was within walking distance), do my shows, walk back, carry nothing in my pockets, and be ready for more Shabbos on Saturday morning.

One Friday night in New Jersey, I was headlining two shows that night and two shows Saturday at a local comedy club: the Main Street Comedy Club in Hackensack (a very desirable place to work for New York comedians because it was a good room [meaning a good venue] and it was twenty minutes away from Manhattan). But I was staying in Teaneck—about three miles away—through the woods. I did my shows Friday night, and left the club to begin my trek back to Teaneck. I got about a block away from the club when the owner pulled up alongside me in his car. We talked about the night, the crowd, we thanked each other, and he asked me where my car was. I told him I didn't have a car. He asked me where I was going. I told him Teaneck. He said, "You don't have a car and you're going to Teaneck?"

I said, "Yes."

He asked me if I wanted a ride to where I was staying, and I said no, I preferred to walk.

He said, "You're walking to Teaneck?"

I said, "Yeah, I feel like walking."

He said, "It's very far away. Get in the car, I'll drive you there."

"Oh, no," I said, "I'll be okay. I like to walk."

He said, "It's twenty degrees outside!"

"Oh, I'll be okay," I answered. "It doesn't feel that cold." (I was freezing!)

He said, "Which road are you taking? The highway to Teaneck is back there!" He pointed in the opposite direction from where I was headed.

I said, "I'm taking a shortcut."

He said, "You're headed toward Parsippany! There's no road to Teaneck there. It's just the woods!"

I said, "Yeah, I know a shortcut ... through the woods."

He said, "You know, that can be pretty dangerous."

I said, "Oh, I'm pretty tough, I'll be okay." Inside I'm thinking, *I'm a dead man!*

He laughed a bit, wished me luck, and said he'd hoped he'd see me the next night.

I said, "Thanks." And inside I was hoping that he would, indeed, be able to see me alive for the Saturday night shows as well.

I stormed through the woods ... on the bridges over the creeks, the roads, the paths, the brush, and I finally, somehow, made it to Teaneck. I might have wound up in Trenton. Who knew. I felt like Tecumseh. I followed the moss on the trees, I listened to the ground to hear the sounds of wagon wheels, I looked for smoke signals, and finally I saw fit to end my frontier tracking skills; I saw a sign reading *Teaneck*. I had made it! I found the street where I was staying, found the house, and tiptoed inside. I quietly crept into what they called the guest bedroom, and breathed a sigh of relief. I forgot about the comedy club, the shows, the audiences, the idle talk, and got a good feeling about being safe and sound and out of the woods. But I got a better feeling about the fact that it wasn't Friday night at the comedy club anymore. It was Shabbos.

ⅎ ℛ

At the places I would stay when I was away for Shabbos, my hosts would always be very cordial folks who were happy to offer their home to a fellow Jew for the Sabbath. The contact would usually be made by my rabbi or a friend. Hospitality amongst Jews is a *mitzvah*. My hosts would always make me feel as comfortable as could be, but most of the time, they had a slew of children and a limited amount of rooms. Yes, slew, meaning a lot! And, yes, limited number of rooms meaning not so many!

So Friday afternoons I would find myself sitting on a twin bed—in that week's infant's bedroom—the aforementioned, guest bedroom—under a constantly turning mobile of ducks, clowns and airplanes. The whole thing smacked of being born again, in an all-too-literal sense. It wouldn't have been so bad if I could've somehow convinced my hosts to support me while their wide-eyed toddler and I went through these formative years together. But I could somehow never fit that into any conversation.

I would put my garment bag on the back of the door and lie down on the twin bed to watch the ceiling calliope dazzle the kid—and me. Why a twin bed is called *twin* I'll never know. The bed is most definitely for only one person; twins would surely have to make other arrangements.

I remember thinking it was a very comforting feeling, and impressive, that strangers would let me sleep in their six-month-old's room on Shabbos without having the slightest idea who I was other than a fellow Jew wanting to re-connect to his Judaism. I felt obliged, of course, in our tradition, to provide hospitality to another Jew at some future time when I could.

Shabbos was approaching. When I couldn't walk to the comedy club, my host family would pack up a Shabbos dinner for me and drive me to a shul within comfortable walking distance of the comedy club, with enough time for my host to drive back before sundown. Before we would leave, I would look around the tiny, dimly lit baby's room decorated with pictures and drawings of ancient Temple finery along with pictures of baseball players and bobble-head figures, and the hypnotizing merry-go-round mobile. I would look at this circus going on, take a look at the baby, look at the circus again, then back to the baby; and at that moment I would realize that that six-month-old infant was in a better position, Jewishly, than I was. Of course, growing up in a home where the television was on nearly twelve hours a day gave me a more thorough understanding of the general *situation comedy* format than this child could ever have. I would soon begin to re-think even this aspect of my life, my long-held, deep-rooted knowledge of things that meant absolutely nothing. I would let out a slight sigh, stand up to open my garment bag, and when I would hit my head on the revolving mobile of ducks and clowns, all I could manage to say was ... *Goo-goo.*

ℰ ℭ

Becoming savvy to the requirements of Jewish observance is not easy. If you start from birth, like I felt I was doing in those crib dens, it's much easier. I would meet a different family each week, a different baby, and a different ceiling mobile. When my accommodation was in an adult-type room, I actually missed the twirling mobile! I still found myself saying goo-goo though.... (Why forgo that?)

Getting used to lighting a Shabbos candle (which is usually specifically done by women and girls) or saying blessings before and after eating, might be tougher to start to do as an adult, but it can be appreciated so much more as something we consciously decide to do solely on our own.

Re-arranging things: going to synagogues, eating only kosher food, prayer, ritual, order—it's all about learning new ways (or sometimes simply remembering). And it's nothing more than deciding to see what it's all about.

I rolled up my sleeves and got started. Some of it was tough, some of it was not. All of it was quite fascinating. Anything worthwhile takes commitment and effort. Acquiring and protecting a precious stone is more difficult than acquiring and protecting a piece of wood. The stakes are higher.

And Then Another Door

At Lincoln Square Synagogue someone told me of a *Tanya* class taught by a Rabbi Kasriel Kastel, a Chabad-Lubavitch rabbi, and program director of Lubavitch Youth Organization. I didn't know what Tanya was at the time. I thought it might be a class about a woman named Tanya. As I mentioned before, the writing, in part, is concerned with the battle between our G-dly soul and our animal soul, and which controls which. (Of course, by studying the work in a class, the G-dly soul has a very good chance of winning.) I loved the class right from day one. The work was fascinating, and Rabbi Kastel's knowledge and sense of humor made it a double-incentive.

So far I had met two Chabad rabbis: Rabbi Kugel and Rabbi Kastel. Once, Rabbi Kastel invited me to Crown Heights in Brooklyn for a Rosh Hashanah. I was scared to go. Too much Chassidic stuff! But Rabbi Kastel convinced me. The world headquarters of Chabad-Lubavitch is located in Crown Heights where the Lubavitcher Rebbe, Menachem Mendel Schneerson, OBM, lived and led that Chassidic movement. And through the Rebbe's teachings and never-ending spiritual presence, is still looked upon as Chabad's leader. I went to Crown Heights, and I loved it. I was made to feel as comfortable as could be and, most importantly to me, people laughed when I said something funny! These were my kind of people! Black hats, black coats, long beards ... who am I kidding, these weren't my kind of people, they were their own kind of people! But I somehow fit in, certainly as a fellow Jew—but, it seemed, more than that.

A few months later I attended what's known as a Shabbaton Weekend in Crown Heights—a gathering of Jews from all over the country and the world. On that Saturday night we viewed a documentary about the Lubavitcher Rebbe.... The Rebbe was born in Ukraine, in Nikolaev, near Odessa. When the Rebbe was five years old, the family moved to a city called Yekatrinislav where his father was the chief rabbi. When I heard the name Yekatrinislav, I paused for a moment. I knew that name.

I knew that name because it was mentioned in my house all the time. My mother happened to have been born in Yekatrinislav ... as were my grandparents and my great-grandparents.

So far, every time I met a Chabad rabbi, there was a coincidence! I was beginning to believe more and more in these coincidences ... and less and less in the *heebee jeebees*. And then I met another very special Chabad rabbi in Manhattan who made a difference to me, Rabbi Benny Krasnianski. There were no coincidences involved here so, as you could imagine, I was quite relieved! It reinforced the commonly held notion that some things happen simply by chance. Uh-oh. There go those *heebee jeebees* again.

₭ ℓ

And so, I was beginning to believe that the new home I was building for myself had already been built.... All I had to do was to move in, and keep looking and finding.

Rabbi Kastel became a dear friend and mentor, and I hope he always will be. (Rabbis Kugel and Krasnianski also, I hope, will be lifelong friends and mentors). And like every new venture, starting on a path of finding my foundation of Judaism again was a matter of walking through doors. Not every door opens, but I was amazed, and still am, at what doors do.

Epilogue

In college, my friends and I once went to the beach at Riis Park in Brooklyn. It was a very hot day, and many people were in the water. The ocean was calm and we were able to stand up in the water, for even a nice distance from the shore, with the water only up to our waists. As we cooled off in the water, bobbing up and down, talking for a good long while, we noticed three or four lifeguards running toward us frantically. Our instincts, of course, were to look behind us, to see who they might be running toward. And when we saw nobody, we all looked at each other—without even an inkling of panic—and then looked at the crazed lifeguards rushing toward us in the water. We instinctively looked around again to see who they could possibly be heading for, and when we again saw nobody behind us or, now, for that matter, in front of us either, we realized they were headed toward us!

We couldn't imagine what they were doing! All we could think of was that it must have been some sort of training exercise. And then we looked around again, and wondered, now with certainly a little more concern, where everybody else who had been in the water with us was!

Just then the lifeguards pounced on us! Grabbing each of us in a life-saver hold, hurriedly taking us, almost dragging us, back to shore. Since we could pretty much stand on our own in the somewhat shallow water, we still couldn't understand what any of this was all about. When we finally made it to shore, we suddenly realized that the beach where we had started from was way down the beach from where we were now!

What happened was that we had gotten caught in a very real rip current that would have surely dragged us slowly out to sea. We couldn't feel anything, didn't realize any sensation of moving, and the only time we got an inkling that anything was amiss was when the lifeguards finally brought us in.

℘ ℭ

My observance has gone on now for more than twenty years. I didn't really make it a part of me … it became a part of me. I couldn't find the center in my stand-up act on stage, but I found it in my life.… And that eventually allowed me to find it in my stand-up act later on.

I look forward to meeting everyone reading my book and, of course, everyone else, at one of my stand-up comedy shows, and certainly fellow Jews at appearances for Jewish organizations where I also perform stand-up comedy, and talk about the story of my return to my Judaism in my show *Comedy and Coming Home*.

Reading about a person is one thing, seeing and talking to that person is another. Getting out in the field is where the fun of performing is; writing is a different kind of fun. Thank you for allow-ing me to share my thoughts and feelings about my Judaism.

And I hope you agree ... where my story continues is not as important as where your story begins.

www.ingramcontent.com/pod-product-compliance
Lightning Source LLC
Chambersburg PA
CBHW031844090426
42741CB00005B/352